HWANGE

ELEPHANT COUNTRY

ZIMBABWE

AFRICAN PUBLISHING GROUP
PO Box BW 350, Harare
ZIMBABWE

© David Martin, Pictures as credited, Maps and Published edition APG

Photographic credits. All David Martin except page 57, Viv Wilson, 59, Peter Ginn, and 61, Gregory Rasmussen.

ISBN: 0-7974-1667-6

Design Paul Wade, Ink Spots, Harare

Printed by Cannon Press, Harare

CONTENTS

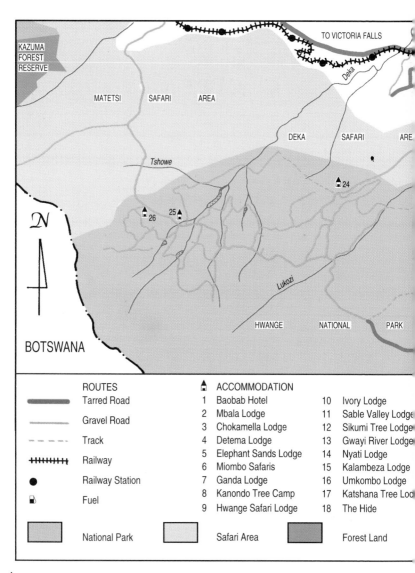

KAZUMA FOREST RESERVE

TO VICTORIA FALLS

Deka

MATETSI   SAFARI   AREA

DEKA   SAFARI   ARE

Tshowe

24

26   25

𝒩

Lukozi

HWANGE   NATIONAL   PARK

BOTSWANA

	ROUTES			ACCOMMODATION		
	Tarred Road		1	Baobab Hotel	10	Ivory Lodge
	Gravel Road		2	Mbala Lodge	11	Sable Valley Lodge
			3	Chokamella Lodge	12	Sikumi Tree Lodge
	Track		4	Detema Lodge	13	Gwayi River Lodge
	Railway		5	Elephant Sands Lodge	14	Nyati Lodge
			6	Miombo Safaris	15	Kalambeza Lodge
	Railway Station		7	Ganda Lodge	16	Umkombo Lodge
	Fuel		8	Kanondo Tree Camp	17	Katshana Tree Lodge
			9	Hwange Safari Lodge	18	The Hide

National Park   Safari Area   Forest Land

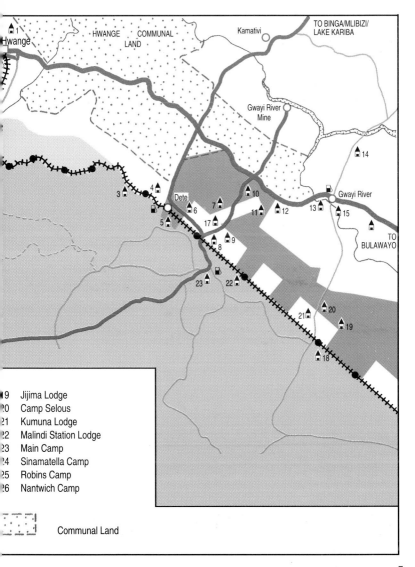

19 Jijima Lodge
20 Camp Selous
21 Kumuna Lodge
22 Malindi Station Lodge
23 Main Camp
24 Sinamatella Camp
25 Robins Camp
26 Nantwich Camp

Communal Land

ACKNOWLEDGEMENTS

This Guide, one of a dozen area-specific Guides about Zimbabwe, was largely researched, written and photographed during a three -week visit to Hwange.

I am particularly indebted to Tish Lee, Anita Maseko and all the staff at Hwange Safari Lodge for their warm hospitality during my stay, which made Room 307 seem like a home away from home.

Two particular human species deserve special mention — Lionel Reynolds and Debbie Grant of Touch the Wild. Lionel is the finest guide to the bush I have ever met and Debbie gave me insights into the very special Presidential elephant herd.

The precolonial and colonial history sections were largely extracted from the excellent M.Phil. work on the northwest of Zimbabwe by Godfrey Ncube of the University of Zimbabwe History Department.

Simuki Chihanga guided me around the imposing Wankie Colliery and Ivan Muramberiwa of Zimbabwe National Museums and Monuments supplied notes for the archaeological section.

Kit Hustler of Wild Horizon Safaris in Victoria Falls, who is acknowledged as one of the region's outstanding ornithologists, produced the bird section and checklist with the help of Peter Ginn, another of Zimbabwe's well-known ornithologists. Meg Coates Palgrave oversaw the section on flora, providing the checklist.

Daryl Martyn, a guide at The Hide, produced the section on butterflies, and Gregory Rasmussen, head of the Painted Dog Research Project, who is known locally as "Mr Dog", focused on his second love to help with the reptile section.

I am also grateful to Chief Wange, Yvonne Steinberg, Viv Wilson, David Brightman, Dr Linley Lister, Maurice Wood and Phyllis Johnson for their support and encouragement.

Finally I am grateful to Zimbabwe Sun Hotels, Touch the Wild, Wild Horizons (Jijima), The Hide and United Touring company, for their support.

David Martin
Hwange

INTRODUCTION

Game viewing, like life, has a lot to do with luck. One day you may visit a waterhole or drive a road and see nothing. On the next day you may encounter a wide variety of animals.

But much of your luck you can make yourself. In part you can do this by properly preparing for your African safari. And once you have arrived there are certain things you can do to maximise the value you get from your visit.

One of the first things to consider is the climate where you are going. In Hwange, in common with Zimbabwe generally, it is cold in June, July and August. Even though you are in Africa the temperature can fall several degrees below freezing point. So bring warm clothes — a sweater, and zip-up jacket, even gloves for the chilly mornings, evenings and nights.

Safari vehicles, at the visitors' request, have been designed to provide maximum visibility. But this has one drawback with visitors subjected to the extremes of cold and heat, dust, rain, and insects. Blankets somewhat alleviate the cold but it is safer to come prepared.

Visitors view elephants from a safari vehicle.

From November through April it rains — or it should — so you will need light protective clothing. In the other months it is warm to hot but the temperature can still drop sharply at night.

Sturdy walking shoes are a necessity but, if they are new, break them in before travelling to avoid blisters. You will notice that your guides and many locals do not wear socks with shoes. This is not local affectation. It is to prevent grass seeds getting into socks, rubbing, and possibly turning septic.

Long trousers are advised to protect your legs against thorns in the bush and the colour of all your clothes should be on the dark side, particularly during walks, so you blend in with your environment.

A hat to protect you against the sun, which can be harsh for those unaccustomed to it, is also advised as are good sunglasses and sun cream. Many people also carry insect repellents. The air, during winter months, can be very dry and skin creams are recommended.

Try to keep the clothing you pack to a practical minimum. If you do not, the unnecessary items will become a burden. Most safari camps provide a same-day laundry service, so clothes cleaned and rotated over a three-day period should be adequate.

One essential bush item many visitors do not bring is binoculars. These will greatly enhance the quality of your viewing of mammals, birds, insects and the flora. There are many types of binoculars available and they can be expensive so borrowing from a friend may be the cheapest means of obtaining them.

Binoculars that give you a 7 x 35 or 8 x 40 magnification, or even lightweight opera glasses, should do. Keep them handy at all times and scan the bush, slowly and carefully, particularly at dawn and dusk. If you reverse your binoculars you can use them as a magnifying glass to get close-ups of insects, butterflies, flowers and grassheads and you will be amazed by the colours you capture.

Cameras, video or still, tend to be much more problematic and a matter of personal choice and pocket. I would advise a minimum of a good camera body of your choice with a standard lens and a 75-300 mm zoom as your workhorse.

Whilst most main brands of films and batteries are available locally, it is as well to carry with you an adequate supply of both, particularly of rechargeable batteries for videos, as few safari camps have recharging facilities.

A camera cleaning kit, at least a blower and brush, is essential. Africa, particularly during the dry season, is very dusty and regular cleaning of your camera equipment will minimise the possibility of scratched film or cameras seizing. Keeping films and batteries in a fridge or freezer, which almost all safari camps have, increases their life.

Another tip which will help you keep your camera steady is a bean bag or something of that sort. Place the bag somewhere steady, rest the lens on the bag and, if it is safe, ensure the engine of your vehicle is turned off and that fellow passengers keep still to minimise vibration.

One further important item to carry with you is a torch. It does not need to be very big but it should be powerful. You will find this an essential item when venturing out of your tent at night at safari camps, some of which do not have mains electricity or generators.

Your health is likely to be another matter which concerns you as you plan your journey. Malaria is common and widespread in Zimbabwe so consult your doctor regarding prophylactics. Personally, I prefer a stronger weekly tablet which minimises the chances of forgetting and of the unpleasant taste.

Water is generally reliable and treated, but you will be advised to check this with your guide wherever you stay. Most camps have septic tanks and maintain high standards of hygiene, which includes washing vegetables, so salads should be safe. But do remember your system is not as acclimatised as those of us who live locally.

So having kitted yourself out you now arrive at your safari destination. The first rule is not to feel inhibited about asking questions. You want to know the highlights, the specialities of the area where you are. You are the paying customer and it is your right to obtain the maximum for what you have paid.

In Zimbabwe the guides you will encounter all hold licences and are trained and examined to very high and demanding standards. Guides who take you on walks are armed for your protection. Always follow their instructions.

They enjoy questions even though, sometimes, regarding a particular tree, bird, insect or butterfly, they may not have a ready answer. LBJ's (little brown jobs) are particularly challenging among Zimbabwe's 650 plus bird species. If your guide cannot answer a question then it is, or should be, a challenge to him/her.

"There is no such thing as a silly question," said Lionel Reynolds, a seasoned guide at Touch the Wild, who examines and trains younger guides. "There are only silly answers."

Africa has a special tempo. You cannot maximise your visit by trying to rush things. You need to relax, forget the office and telephone, adjust to that special pace. That way you will see and feel more.

In broad terms the African day can be broken into three parts — dawn, midday and dusk. What you see, hear, smell and sense, varies throughout this day.

DAWN
The dawn drive is generally the time to look for predators such as lions and leopards who may have killed during the night. Getting up and out early is important to the success of this. Likely you will have paid a lot of money for what you are about to see and you will see nothing by staying in your hotel room.

Don't expect to find large herds on this drive. They will still be sheltering in the bush. Listen to the early morning sounds such as bird songs; enjoy the dawn light, and watch for unusual activity.

This unusual activity — and the signs — includes lion or leopard tracks on the road. Carnivores frequently use the main roads in preference to wet or dewy grass and the bush which their cubs have difficulty navigating. There may also be drag marks where they have pulled their kill into the shade. Jackal and hyena may be hanging around to share a kill although both are predators in their own right as well as scavengers and opportunists.

Other evidence of the drama of the kill could be around. Vultures will not be on the wing so early. They wait for the temperature to increase, generating the thermals upon which they rise. But a concentration of vultures in a given tree or area could suggest they are awaiting their turn from an earlier kill.

Brown Snake Eagles and Bateleur Eagles, who do not have to wait for the thermals, and who serve as a marker for the subsequent arrival of the vultures, are another early morning sign to look for.

Lion.

Also look for the signs in other animals such as impala, wildebeest and zebra. If they are tense, bunching, or looking in one direction ignoring your presence, this may mean a predator is not far away.

Look carefully at waterholes and "glass" the surrounding bush (this is where your binoculars are vital), especially during the dry season. Carefully check termite mounds and other places where lions, satiated on an overnight kill or simply watching, may be sunning themselves.

During the early morning look mainly at the ground, peering through, rather than at, the surrounding bush. You are looking for silhouettes and shadows, for anything that seems somewhat out of place or moves, perhaps a lion's ear or leopard's tail. Maybe the unusual will be a termite mound, a bush or a log. Sometimes it will be a predator.

MIDDAY
In this period, which in winter months can be more productive than early mornings (and certainly warmer), you can ask your guide to be taken to a hide, a water hole, or the shade of a tree, where you can picnic. Silence and keeping still will yield the most rewarding results.

In the heat of the day, antelope and birds will come to a waterhole. Your inconspicuous presence will give you the opportunity to observe the animals' and birds' behaviour — whether they approach the water

11

in columns, singly or in large groups, how they drink, whether they leave one of their number as a sentinel, who dominates the species and which dominates another.

This is an opportunity to look beyond the big mammals for the small things which complete the African cycle.

And after lunch most species — including guides — need a siesta to sharpen their senses for the final climactic phase of the African day.

DUSK

This period for most who live in the bush is the highlight of the day. It is when you are most likely to see and observe the biomass of animals and that very special soft and unforgettable African twilight which, particularly towards the end of the dry season, swiftly gives way to brilliant red sunsets.

It is also the time of day to drive particularly slowly, to savour the magic around you, to focus. Settle down, watch, listen and observe.

You will not see more, and you will likely see less, by driving at excessive speed. And don't drive up to animals quickly to try to get a closer picture or provoke a charge. It is most likely that the animal will rapidly disappear, leaving you with nothing.

Stop at a distance when you see an animal and turn off your engine. Give the animal room and space, do not make it feel threatened by the speed of your vehicle, proximity, or even direct eye contact in the case of lion and baboon, particularly when walking with a guide. Such eye contact makes them feel threatened.

Let the animal relax and get used to your presence. Then, very slowly, move closer, preferably obliquely and cautiously. Avoid sudden movements and raised voices. Create an empathy with the animal and the environment. That way you will maximise your viewing.

The animal, out of curiosity, may decide on its own to move closer to you, to check you out. Generally you can feel fairly safe. I have photographed elephants from a vehicle from less than six feet away once they realised I was not a threat.

Remember always not to rush Africa and the mammals that live in it. It is there to savour and, like a good wine, the true flavour is more pronounced and enjoyable when tasted slowly.

At the end of your Introduction to the ways and wiles of Africa there are a few definite "don'ts". But these, for your own benefit and the benefit of others, are positive and not negative.

Always try to be considerate of others, be they the animals, the environment or fellow humans. Exceeding speed limits (40 km/h in Hwange and most places) endangers animals, other road users and throws up clouds of dust. You will see more game if you travel slowly and look carefully.

If you happen upon a particular species, take your pictures and move on making room for others. Do not get out of vehicles, these are wild animals and such threatening behaviour towards them can place you and others in danger. Beware of starting fires; the place for cigarette ends and litter is in your vehicle to be disposed of later.

Don't be obsessive about seeing a given species or you will preclude yourself seeing many other things. And always remember that you, yourself, are in Africa, not at a zoo, safari park, or viewing a film about Africa and its wildlife on your TV from your favourite armchair. What you are seeing is the real Africa.

13

GEOLOGY

Geologically, the rock strata of Hwange District can be divided into three parts, the youngest of which — Kalahari sand — covers around 90 per cent of the surface of Hwange National Park.

The first era is what geologists refer to as Basement, the bottom, as the word implies, or oldest strata of the region. Over this lie the other identified strata.

The gneisses of the Basement are 2,600 to 3,300 million years old and were created by molten rock squeezed up from the earth's mantle crystallising below the surface and then being subjected to heat and pressure.

Above this comes the Karroo System. This is dated as being 150 to 300 million years old. Within the Karroo System, which is scattered from Port Elizabeth to Kenya, coal evolved some 200 million years ago.

Today, coal, which is simply ancient wood, exists in large quantities and is mined in the Hwange town area. Fossilised wood can be seen in some parts of the Hwange National Park.

The top of the Karroo System is marked by flows of basalt which

Fossil Trees

The Deteema vlei (an Afrikaans word meaning hollow where water collects during the rains) in Hwange National Park is one of more than 20 locations in Zimbabwe where fossilised logs and forests can be found.

If visitors take the short road to Deteema picnic site they pass through the middle of a fossilised forest area. At the site itself fossilised logs are on display.

Fossil wood is wood that has undergone silification meaning that the original wood substance has been replaced by sodium silicate which is resistent to cold, heat, water, and the passage of electricity.

Some 200 million years ago, a species of conifer covered the Zambezi Valley and it is the fossil remains of these forests which are now found in the Karroo sediment in areas such as Hwange.

poured across the ground surface as volcanic lava around 150 million years ago. This is the early Jurassic Period. But, before anyone goes looking for huge footprints or massive bones, dinosaurs are not known to have inhabited this area.

Basalt occurs most commonly around the Victoria Falls area and to the south of Hwange National Park where the rivers have eroded their way downwards through the overlying Kalahari System.

The Kalahari System, more commonly known as Kalahari sand, once covered much of Zimbabwe. This blanket of sand stretched three-quarters of the way across the country and today pockets of it can be found as far east as Mvuma on the Harare to Masvingo road.

The sand was blown from Botswana and deposited across Zimbabwe, beginning 12 to 15 million years ago. This spasmodic "sandstorm" lasted until about one million years ago and geologists have estimated that some Hwange dunes were once as high as 80 m.

Today, in the southern part of the Hwange National Park, dunes still exist. But they have been eroded down to no more than 10 m in height. Over the last million years the sand has gradually been eroded with pockets of basalt re-emerging as the Kalahari cover diminished.

Sand is basically small particles of quartz, which can be white, yellow or red depending upon which other chemicals such as iron oxide have been incorporated.

The three National Parks camps are located in differing geological areas although this had more to do with water availability than planned tourist variation.

Main Camp is situated on the eastern fringe of Zimbabwe's largest Kalahari sand deposit, Robins Camp to the northwest on basalt, and Sinamatella in the north-centre on the Karroo System sedimentary rocks.

ARCHAEOLOGY

From the limited evidence to date it is known that our ancestors flourished in this area between 80,000 and 100,000 years ago.

But, in contrast with the Matobos near Bulawayo, and Eastern Zambia, the Late Stone Age period has not been thoroughly investigated in the Hwange area.

The stone tools found at the Bumbusi Ruins site have been dated at between 14,000 and 20,000 years old.

Bumbusi Ruins themselves are much more recent, built around 1834. It was the second capital (the first being at Shangano) of Chief Wange and the Nambya people.

Bumbusi Ruins.

The little that is known is best represented at Bumbusi Ruins by the rock engravings. These sandstone engravings depict the spoor of lion, buffalo, giraffe, zebra, roan, sable, impala, warthog and quagga, a now extinct wild ass related to the zebra.

Bumbusi Ruins are located in the bush close to a rough road, one hour's drive from Sinamatella Camp. Because they are within a national park, they fall under the Department of National Parks which shows little or no interest in preserving and publicising them.

Even finding them can be difficult. A senior ranger from

Sinamatella who accompanied me, had never visited the Bumbusi site before. He neglected to bring a gun, which is essential on a walk (we disturbed five buffalo), and he knew nothing about the area's history having originated in another part of Zimbabwe.

An older Nambya worker from Sinamatella accompanied us and he had some knowledge of the area and its history. He told us that National Parks had denied the Nambya people access to the site for 20 years for their rain ceremony which is supposed to be done annually. One could not help but wonder about the significance of this when measured against the area's deteriorating rainfall!

Tsoro

The popular local board game, Tsoro, is not unique to Zimbabwe. In East Africa it is known as Bao and it is played throughout the continent as well as in Asia, Indonesia, the Philippines and southern China. In West Africa the game is variously called Wari, Songe and Mankala and in Ethiopia, where it is most commonly known as Sabata or Sadega, 103 name variations have been recorded.

Archaeologists have dated boards cut into rock back to  the 1st century and in Ethiopia two row games carved in stone have been dated to the 6th and 7th centuries. The boards themselves vary. Some have four rows of holes, others six. And the number of holes in each row on a board can vary from six to ten. Seeds, stones or shells are normally used as counters.

In one method of playing the game three counters are placed in each hole. The counters are then distributed, one per hole, by the first player in a clockwise direction beginning at the first hole after the pickup. The process is repeated until the player reaches an empty hole. Then it is the other player's turn.

The objective is to win as many counters as possible from the opponent's side. This is either done through emptying your opponent's side of counters or removing those with four in a hole on another player's side and counting who has the most at the end.

The sandstone engravings depicting animal spoor are to be found in caves just off the road approaching Bumbusi. And on several rocks in the area, Tsoro (a variant of checkers or drafts) boards are carved where, presumably, sentries once whiled away the hours whilst watching for human and mammal intruders.

Free-standing rock-walls without any form of cement to hold them together are scattered over a large area. On the largest *kopje* (rock outcrop) where the Nambya chief is believed to have lived, they are built between natural rock into the steep sides one ascends and on the top around the area where the chief's house was built.

Elsewhere in the area one finds these remarkably architected stone structures on *kopjes,* which appear to indicate where senior Nambya lived.

Nearby are the remains of the Nambya iron foundry which the guide only found with difficulty. This was built around 1850 and part of the chimney still stands.

Baboons and other animals — and the environment — are progressively taking their toll on what remains of the Bumbusi Ruins which are ignored and neglected.

Those who have walked parts of Hwange National Park say there is a remarkable amount of evidence of other *mazimbabwe* (houses of stone) and human settlement in the area. But such archaeological and historical treasures remain known to few and face the very real danger of being lost for all time.

Walls and original baobab at Bumbusi.

HISTORY

The first known Bantu-speakers in the Hwange area were the Kalundu group whom the earliest archaeological evidence indicates inhabited the area between AD 400 and 500 with their occupancy peaking around AD 800.

Occupations by a series of groups followed with the Tonga moving south from Zambia into northwestern Zimbabwe in search of perennial water in the 11th and 12th centuries.

Tonga movement southwards was halted by the northerly migrations and conquests of Shona groups causing the Tonga to withdraw into the Zambezi Valley and southern Zambia where they live today.

Another group originating in Zambia, the Leya, occupied much of the area in which Hwange is now incorporated. Although no specific date has been established for their arrival, they initially settled in the Victoria Falls area before expanding their influence to the south and southeast.

Thereafter the history of the area becomes more detailed. Early in the 18th century, Dende, one of the three sons of the Rozvi Changamire (king or leader), broke away from his father to establish himself as an independent ruler in present-day northwestern Zimbabwe.

Dende's actions are said to have infuriated the Rozvi Changamire who gave orders that his son be captured and killed.

Dende's actions in this period strongly suggest he felt in danger. He swiftly moved ever further away from his father, stopping briefly in several places, and strengthening kinship ties through leaving behind sisters who married Tonga men.

Three times he changed his name — from Dende to Sawanga and finally to Wange (said to be an abbreviation of his previous name) which became the hereditary dynastic title.

Chief Wange

Chief Wange, aged 74, became the 13th leader of the Nambya people 22 years ago. He lives on a smallholding 20 km from Hwange town.

Dende, and his followers, a patrilineal people of the *soko* (monkey) totem who were later known as Nambya, entered the Leya territory via Lower Gwayi, settling in the Bhale area between the Gwayi, Nyantuwe and Lukosi rivers. Here they assimilated some of the Leya who had not resisted their incorporation into the Nambya State.

On top of a strategic hill named Shangano (deriving from the Nambya word *shangana* meaning "meet") they built a stone-walled enclosure which became the first capital of their State.

The Nambya are believed to have moved from Shangano to the Bumbusi area in the upper Deka valley during the reign of the fifth Wange, Shana (1834-60). In large measure the move appears to have been dictated by the greater suitability of the wetter soil at Bumbusi for bulrush millet, sorghum and maize which were Nambya staples.

The new capital was sited on a rocky promontory beneath two large baobab trees which still stand. The stone-walled enclosure was about 55 metres long and two metres high and the royal dwellings were located within this complex.

The masonry on the walls was a variant of the architecture of Great Zimbabwe and the Nambya *mazimbabwe* (houses of stone), like the many other *mazimbabwe* scattered throughout the country, is believed to have been built primarily to symbolise wealth, prestige and authority of the ruling class.

While the Nambya were a patrilineal people, one school of thought speculates that their inter-action with, and assimilation of, the Tonga and Leya, who are both matrilineal, may have influenced Nambya successions.

This pivotal role may, one interpretation argues, explain the succession of the sixth Wange, Lusambami, whose mother, Bakwimbe, was the sister of the late Shana and who ensured the succession of her son over Shana's oldest son, Mpalazhuji, becoming the next Wange.

But it may also indicate the degree to which the matrilineal ideology of the Leya and Tonga had come to the fore as the family tree of the Wange dynasty shows two more heirs emerging from the female line between 1853 and 1904.

Before a successor to a deceased Wange is appointed the dynasty's senior women *(bakwegulu)* assemble and the legitimate heir is adorned with a string of beads, handed down from the previous Wange, as the symbol of office.

At the installation the new Wange is offered soil to symbolise his custodianship of the land by the deceased Wange's sister *Netenje* (her dynastic title) who plays the pivotal role in this ceremony.

However, a second explanation may be advanced. Such a succession process was similar to that in the Mutapa state which covered much of Zimbabwe from 1400 - 1900. Mutapa succession was not from father to the eldest son of the late ruler but passed to nephews and cousins in a specific order. Though patrilineal, the wives and sisters also played a pivotal role in the Mutapa State successions.

In common with several groups in the region, the Nambya believe in the existence of the spirits of their deceased ancestors and practise a variation of ancestor worship. They believe in immortality, with spirit mediums *(mande)* acting as go-betweens in communicating between the spirits of the dead and the living. Most mediums are women.

The advent of the agricultural season is marked by a village rain-making ceremony *(miliya)* conducted at the graveside of the immediate relative by the village headman *(ishe)*. Beer is brewed and this, watered down, poured on the grave while a good rainy season is asked for.

If the rains fail to arrive by January, which today is not uncommon in the Hwange area, and drought is threatened, the elders *(vashe)* conduct a national rain-making ceremony at the graves of previous Wanges.

At each ceremony a black sheep is slaughtered, roasted and eaten with some meat offered to the ancestor Wange by being placed beside his grave. Beer mixed with water is again poured on the grave.

Since the graves of the first three Wanges are so far apart, and since the ceremony should be conducted at all of them, this larger "national" ceremony involves travelling considerable distances.

A well-organised economic and social structure existed among the Nambya well before the Ndebele raids of 1850 and after, the southwards advance of tsetse fly which made cattle-keeping impossible in the area, the introduction of firearms, the importation of European goods, and intensive hunting from 1860.

Agriculture, followed by animal husbandry, hunting, gathering, fishing and manufacturing, underpinned the society.

The crops grown, and the techniques used to grow them, ensured the area was more or less self-sufficient and provides a salutary lesson to those who today talk about resistant crops to combat drought.

Cattle, once a social asset, a source of protein, a manifestation of wealth used in marriage transactions *(lobola),* and an item to barter during periods of crop deficit, inevitably diminished in importance after the arrival of the tsetse fly in the area.

Hitherto, cattle had been at the core of Nambya culture as was the case with several other groups. If the importance of cattle disappeared then part of the culture was lost.

The Nambya now turned to smaller stock such as sheep and goats to barter to combat crop deficits. Goats in turn brought environmental degradation.

Hunting, gathering (insects, fruit, leaves, roots, wild grasses and honey) and fishing were subsidiary pursuits yet they provided additional insurance in times of shortage. The hunting of big game, a dangerous pursuit, was usually a village or communal pursuit while smaller game was hunted by individuals.

Nambya hunters were noted as skilful trackers who would variously employ bows and arrows, spears (the Nambya tipped their spears with a poison drawn from a bulb called *chenyami*), and traps to catch their prey.

The methods of fishing depended upon the season and water level. In the summer months when the rivers flooded, fish were trapped behind reed barriers. In the drier months, ponds were poisoned to stupefy the fish which then surfaced and were scooped up. Fish traps, allowing entry but denying exit, were also employed as were spearing and fish hooks. But the catch was poor.

The Nambya environment, with its isolated pockets suitable for cultivation, led them (like the Tonga) to practice extensively what is today officially much condemned and called riverbank cultivation. Bulrush millet was their staple crop followed by sorghum and maize. There are also eyewitness accounts of Nambya cotton cultivation, also an economic activity of the Mutapa State.

Crop damage and loss from hippo, elephant, buffalo, antelope, warthog and baboon was a continual hazard with lookout platforms erected on the edge of cultivated fields. Guards would shout and blow on charmed whistles and horns to chase off marauding animals. In other cases fires were lit at night and scarecrows used to chase away grain-eating birds.

Thus hunting served a twofold purpose — the protection of crops through reducing the threat from wild animals and as meat for the pot.

Locusts posed another serious problem. Local methods of controlling them, largely aimed at ridding a single threatened field of the "hoppers", were ineffectual and only the introduction of spraying in the 1930s began to control this threat.

Archaeological, oral and documentary evidence also shows that iron-smelting and smithing was widely practised. The largest Nambya forge and furnace was at Bumbusi. It had a long chimney on one side and forge on the other and the ruins of this still exist at Bumbusi in Hwange National Park.

Salt was extracted from salt pans through evaporation, and

Bumbusi chimney.

23

traded. A slow and embryonic cotton industry wove cloth on clay cotton-whorls from the crops cultivated, and tobacco was processed and traded to be smoked in clay pipes and as snuff.

Labour in most endeavours was a household responsibility. Men, for instance, cut the timber and built the house frames, women cut the thatch and collected the *daga* (mud) to plaster walls. Men cleared the bush for cultivation, felling trees and burning them, and wives and daughters planted the crops. More dangerous pursuits, such as guarding fields and hunting larger animals, were usually male preserves.

The second half of the 19th century brought considerable changes for the Nambya people. Broadly, these changes were brought about by two quite different factors, one resulting from the *mfecane* (a Zulu word literally meaning "the crushing"), and the other by the arrival of European traders and settlers.

These two events radically changed the political, economic and social structure which existed in Nambya society.

The first group of European traders to reach the area are thought to have been the Portuguese and their African agents, the Chikunda, who originated in Mozambique. These Portuguese were involved in the slave and ivory trade and, hitherto, had been thought to have reached the area by canoe from the east up the Zambezi Valley from Quelimane in Mozambique via Kariba.

However, there is now reason to believe that the earliest Portuguese reached the area from the Atlantic coast through Angola and the Ovimbundu areas of today's southern Angola and northern Namibia. Their arrival, some historians now argue, pre-dated 1850 and brings into doubt the contention that Dr David Livingstone was the first white man to see Victoria Falls.

The Portuguese purchased large numbers of young Nambya men and women who were exported as slaves. This trade seriously depleted the Nambya population and following the abolition of the slave trade, the Nambya began purchasing slaves back from the Portuguese in return for ivory as a means of replenishing their population.

The abolition of the slave trade coincided with a substantial increase in the price of ivory used for piano keys, billiard balls, knife handles and ornaments in Europe in the post-industrial revolution. Beads and cloth had been exchanged for ivory (and previously slaves) and

Ovimbundu traders from Angola exchanged hoes for slaves thereby undermining the Nambya textile industry and iron foundries.

The demand for ivory, and its growing scarcity south of the Limpopo River, drew South African hunters to the area from around 1860. They brought with them an alternative source of European goods including, increasingly, guns to barter.

Between 1871 and 1888 the trade took on a more permanent nature with the establishment of a trading post at Pandamatenga by George Westbeach, an expert hunter and trader. This, and other subsequent trading stations, sowed the idea of migrant labourers working in South Africa's mines for money which could be converted into the items hitherto only obtainable from the slave-and-ivory-trading caravans.

The Nambya loose hegemony and comparative peace was shattered by the Ndebele arrival. Their then Chief Wange, Lusumbami, according to all oral accounts, was skinned alive by the Ndebele.

His followers fled, dispersing into smaller mainly family units occupying inaccessible parts of the mountainous country south of the Zambezi River or crossing into Zambia only to return between 1888 and 1893, the latter date marking the defeat of the Ndebele by the British South Africa Company (BSAC) in the Anglo-Ndebele war.

The Nambya were the group most seriously affected by the Ndebele raids, losing their remaining cattle and agricultural lands as well as their Chief and hundreds of their people.

But they managed to retain their cultural identity and government, and the hereditary dynastic title of the Nambya rulers, established over 200 years ago by Dende, continues today with the present Chief Wange being the thirteenth in line.

COLONIAL
As shown in the previous section, the true pioneers of white occupation were in fact the Portuguese who traded in slaves and ivory, as well as missionaries such as Livingstone and Robert Moffat, and hunters like Frederick Courteney Selous.

They were responsible for the rumours of extensive gold deposits in Zimbabwe, and Rhodes' "Pioneer" Column in 1890 merely followed their footsteps searching for El Dorado.

The Nambya who had returned from Zambia, and those who had emerged from their sanctuaries in the hills south of the Zambezi River, were totally deprived of their southern land by the settlers by 1910.

In 1893 a German, Albert Giese, had heard about "black stones that burn". Two years later he pegged 1,036 square km of southern Nambya in the Bumbusi area as a coalfield.

Wankie Colliery

The history of Wankie Colliery started 200 million years ago. The swamp vegetation fringing the inland sea which then existed in the area formed the coal seam which has been mined for 90 years.

German geologist, Albert Giese, heard of "black stones that burn" while in Bechuanaland (now

Botswana) where he worked on a mine. Two years later he began pegging the area laying new foundations for today's colliery.

Conditions for workers in those early days were described as "appalling" as the mine owners sought profits. The original owners went into liquidation and a new company, Wankie Colliery Company Ltd., was formed.

Both profits and conditions gradually improved (a 1972 mine disaster in which 427 people were killed notwithstanding) and today the mine's output is in excess of five million tonnes of coal for industry and farmers as well as coke for export. Several other ancilliary items such as tar are also produced.

Hwange town, owned and run by the company, is a surprisingly large and tidy complex just off the main Bulawayo road 100 km before Victoria Falls. It boasts a modern hospital serving the district, schools, banks, services such as refuse disposal and its own newspaper.

When development of the coal concession began in 1903 all Nambya living in the area were resettled to the east in the Lukosi and Nyantuwe areas.

The railway line (conceived by Rhodes to link the Cape and Cairo) was constructed from Bulawayo to Wankie (now Hwange) in 1903 and on to Victoria Falls the following year, leading to further Nambya land alienation.

Between 1904 and 1909 the land was surveyed for European farming settlement and by 1910 a total of 3,383,800 acres of the best Nambya land, representing 45 per cent of the Wankie District's total, had been taken for the colliery, railway and white farmers.

In 1910 all the Nambya occupying land along the rail from Dete to upper Matetsi, and those on European designated farmland, were removed and resettled in the Lukosi and Nyantuwe area, joining those who had already been removed from the colliery concession area.

The irony was that the Nambya were being resettled in an area they had left 70 years earlier because of its limited agricultural potential, while the potentially more productive farmlands they surrendered to the settlers were to remain largely under-utilised for the next 70 years!

The area to which the Nambya were relegated was rocky, lacked water and had little agriculture potential. Designated as a Native Reserve in 1918, "... nine-tenths would be practically useless, owing to the want of water and rocky nature of the soil", the Native Commissioner observed.

Some Nambya, aware of the crisis on the reserve, refused to move to it, settling on still unalienated land. To try to force the resisters out, the BSAC had introduced a land tax in 1909. This in turn led to overt resistance with Nambya threatening to migrate back to Zambia.

Increased pressure from white farmers for the removal of Africans reached a new crescendo in 1923 and, with the existing reserve already unable to support the population forced to live in it, two more adjoining reserves were created in 1924.

But the land assigned was no better. One reserve was described as "waterless, rocky and barren" by the Native Commissioner and of the other he said he had not seen "poorer land in [Southern] Rhodesia".

By 1925, of the total land in Wankie District, five per cent had been set aside for reserves, 45 per cent was alienated (already taken) and 50 per cent of the area, or a little over 5 million acres, unalienated. This was soon to change for the worse for the Nambya.

In 1928 a total of 4 million acres, just over 93 per cent of the unalienated land, was designated for the Wankie Game Reserve. Nambya still living in this area were forcibly removed to the reserves. The villages of those who resisted were burnt by Southern Rhodesian policemen.

Of the remaining 286,000 acres of unalienated land, most of this was subsequently declared a forest reserve, thereby leaving the Nambya landless outside the three reserves (later reduced to two).

Despite their harsh environment, few Nambya were willing to work in Wankie where by 1962 (nine years after the Anglo-American Company of South Africa had acquired a substantial shareholding), there were 2,000 European men and 18,000 African men mainly working for the colliery and Rhodesia Railways.

The Nambya had been migrating to the South African mines for some 80 years and were aware that these offered better wages than the meagre exploitative wages at Wankie, as well as better health conditions. An estimated 60 per cent of able-bodied men became migrant labourers and as a result Wankie Colliery faced serious labour shortages having to recruit its labourers from Zambia.

Educationally the Nambya also suffered. The Southern Rhodesian government left education to missionaries in Hwange and, because of disease and poor communications, few established themselves in the area. The first primary school opened in 1913 and the first secondary school, even then only for Forms 1 and 2, not until 1962.

While, slowly at first, the Wankie colliery developed a well-equipped hospital, medical facilities elsewhere in the district remained poor to non-existent. Kamativi Tin Mine had only a 12-bed hospital for 1,371 Africans.

Cheap labour meant exactly that and expenditure on education, health, housing, sanitation and diet was minimised with a Southern Rhodesian health inspector in this period describing conditions for Africans as "appalling".

The combination of poor diet, squalid accommodation and high production demands to ensure profits for the mine owners, is estimated to have led to the deaths of 34,000 African mine labourers in Southern Rhodesia between 1900 and 1950.

The depopulation of the Nambya area was to have an environmental impact. Southern Rhodesian legislation tried to disarm Africans and prevent traditional hunting. The result was the unchecked spread of bush, resurgence of tsetse and multiplication of wild animals, particularly predators such as lions.

African resistance to their changing circumstance was manifested through the unwillingness of the Nambya to work for exploitative wages in local Southern Rhodesian industries, avoidance of particular employers (some farmers paid as little as 5 shillings per month), agents of the Southern Rhodesian Native Labour Bureau, job desertion, and frequent strike action.

The depopulation of the area, and the alienation of large areas for the Wankie Game Reserve and for forestry, was to make the northwest of Southern Rhodesia a difficult area for guerrillas to operate in when they began the second *Chimurenga* (war for liberation) in the 1960s.

While the Nambya had been comparatively inactive during the first *Chimurenga* against the white settlers in 1896 (most of them having been driven from Hwange District by the invading Ndebele), they were to play a much greater role during the second *Chimurenga.*

In August 1967, in one of most publicised and epic battles of the Zimbabwean liberation war, a force of 80 guerrillas fought for several days with the Southern Rhodesian security forces. Seven members of the Southern Rhodesian forces were killed and 13 wounded against 30 guerrillas killed, a security forces communique claimed.

The Wankie Battle, as it became known, appropriately brought together African guerrillas from Zimbabwe and South Africa in a battle symbolising unity against the white settlers.

Psychologically, therefore, the Wankie Battle was of great importance. As the war of liberation escalated, tourist facilities in the area became increasingly inaccessible and dangerous. Peace returned to the area when Zimbabwe became independent in 1980.

HWANGE
NATIONAL PARK

Hwange National Park is Zimbabwe's largest park covering 1,460,000 hectares (14,540 square km), roughly the size of Belgium, and it contains the country's largest concentration — and greatest diversity — of animals.

It is located in Matabeleland North Province, with Botswana on its western border, the Matetsi Safari Area in the north, Forestry Commission and private land to the east, and Tjolotjo Communal Lands in the south.

Hwange's physical appearance and activities change with the seasons. The onset of the rains from November gives the park a verdent hue with waterbirds more plentiful and many species giving birth.

April and May, immediately after the rains, coincides with rutting by such species as impala, tsessebe and warthog. In the colder months the days are crisp and clear, before the hot season when the sky becomes hazier as a result of smoke from bush fires.

Hwange straddles a portion of a shallow watershed separating the Zambezi river system, which drains the north and northwest of the park, from the drainage lines which head southwest from Main Camp towards the Makgadikgadi salt pans across the border in Botswana.

The climate is semi-arid with rainfall in the north of the park averaging 620 mm a year and decreasing as one proceeds south towards the fossil drainage lines and fossil dunes running into Botswana.

Fossil drainage lines and dunes are an important facet of Hwange National Park. The fossil drainage beds were once rivers draining into an inland sea which covered the area 13,000 to 18,000 years ago during the last ice age.

These onetime rivers rose in fairly open grassland near the railway line on the park's northeastern boundary and their passage through the park is shown today by the Dete, Main Camp and Kennedy vleis.

There is little permanent water on the Kalahari sands which cover much of Hwange up to a depth of 150 m. This factor, to complement the occasional springs and seeps thereby ensuring a greater mammal presence all year round, necessitated the introduction of some 60 bore-hole-fed seasonal pans. Thus, what one sees in Hwange today is a man-made, albeit well-intentioned, distortion of what might have been — had nature's vagaries and extremes been allowed to take their course. Water remains central to Hwange's management.

Two major vegetation divisions predominate in Hwange. On the shallower soils of the north, northwest and south, mopane woodland dominates. The centre of the park is dominated by mixed scrub interspersed with *vleis* and Kalahari woodland.

Hwange represents a meeting-place for animals from two normally distinct faunal zones. In the park's more arid southwest one finds animals such as gemsbok, hartebeest, wildebeest, brown hyena, bat-eared fox and giraffe who have adapted to these severe conditions. In the north and northwest, animals associated with less severe habitats are more common.

While a number of existing Hwange species are threatened or endangered, only two have become extinct in the past 100 years — the white and black rhino, both highly sensitive to over-hunting and now reintroduced.

In late 1966 and early 1967, 35 white rhino were introduced to Hwange from Natal in South Africa. Today, rarely seen, less than a handful survive in the southern part of the park.

White rhino.

The black rhino population, albeit under heavily armed protection, has fared better with over 50 surviving in thick bush in the north of the park.

MAMMALS

Hwange National Park and surrounds has over 100 recorded species of mammals. But in a short stay lasting only a few days it is most improbable that you will see all of them.

Some are rare, peculiar to a particular area, or nocturnal. At the back of this Guide there is a checklist of the main Hwange species. Here we concentrate on giving you as much background as space permits on the species you are most likely to be interested in and most likely to see.

A number of smaller animals, some of which you may see, such as the bushpig, bushbaby (Galago), scrub hare, spring hare (to be seen hopping like a kangaroo in car lights), hedgehog, pangolin, porcupine and squirrel, have had to be excluded because of space and because this is a Guide, not a mammal book.

For full coverage of the region's mammals I would commend two particular books. These are *The Mammals of the Southern African Subregion* (The University of Pretoria) by J.D Skinner and R.H.N. Smithers, and *Mammals of Zimbabwe* (African Publishing Group, forthcoming) by Viv Wilson.

In Hwange, if for no other reasons than its sheer size and numerical dominance, the elephant must take pride of place.

The day I arrived at Hwange Safari Lodge to write the bulk of this Guide, over 150 elephants, females with calves followed by bulls, raced trumpeting across the far side of the *vlei* opposite the lodge. Apparently they had been disturbed by the sudden drop in temperature and extreme increase in the wind.

Two days later, during a six-hour tour of part the 140-square-km Hwange Estate (controlled by Touch the Wild and Zimbabwe Sun Hotels who own the Hwange Safari Lodge), I saw well over 100 elephants.

Those at SAF Lodge (tour guide jargon for Hwange Safari Lodge), and on the Hwange Estate, are normally members of the Presidential herd which numbers well over 300.

That is only a fraction of the 30,000 elephants estimated to be in the 14,540-square-km Hwange National Park, Matetsi complex, communal and forest areas during the September 1995 aerial survey. Of these, almost 23,000 were in the park and it should be noted that the population for Hwange District is slightly under half the total estimated Zimbabwean national herd.

Next at Hwange, again in size and numerically, comes the buffalo. These you will find in large herds numbering several hundreds or in small all-male groups.

Hippopotamus, in the right location, can also be readily seen although they exist in larger numbers and very much closer proximity in places like the Zambezi River.

The cats — lion, leopard and cheetah — are more problematic. Whilst the visitor is most likely to see lion, usually to be found in prides, the more solitary leopard and cheetah are much harder to find. It is here that luck and patience comes into play.

Giraffe are common, sometimes found in surprisingly large herds, as are the plains game such as zebra, impala and wildebeest. Sable, kudu and eland (these are found in particular areas) can also be seen as can warthog, hyena, squirrel and mongoose.

Elephant
One imported guide book the visitor might encounter states that because the elephant is so well known "no detailed description" is necessary. It would be hard to think of a more fatuous and inaccurate statement.

The origins, history (including misguided economic importance), description, distribution, habitat, behavioural patterns, diet and reproductive cycle of the elephant makes it one of the most fascinating mammals about whom the serious scientist, guide and visitor still craves to know more.

Origins
Elephants belong to the *Elephantidae* family of the *Proboscidea* order. Their earliest ancestor was a small pig-like creature named

Trunk call.

Presidential herd

The Presidential Elephant Herd Research Project on the Hwange Estate adjoining Hwange Safari Lodge began on a fulltime basis in September 1993. Its objectives were to estimate the herd size through individual identification, assess the herd structure and demographics, study social behaviour and vegetation utilisation, including the impact on the area of the elephants, and ascertain the elephant's range.

The Presidential herd was defined as those elephants spending most of their time within the estate, which is jointly run by Hwange Safari Lodge and Touch the Wild, a local safari company, whose managing director, naturalist, and now Member of Parliament for Hwange, Alan Elliott, has been observing them for 20 years.

Elliott employed Debbie Grant, a Zimbabwean honours graduate in zoology, to collect the scientific data. To date she has identified and named 78 cows, 107 calves and 72 bulls which frequent the estate. She has found that there are 11 breeding groups on the estate ranging from six to 40 individuals in number. Sixteen calves were recorded as born between January and November 1995 with November being the highest birth month (as in the previous year) thereby fixing peak conception in January during the rains.

Only 26 years old, Debbie's persistent observation of the herd has earned her the nickname, *Mandlovu*, which in the Sindebele language means Mother Elephant.

Moeritherium. Fossil remains show they lived some 50 million years ago on the swamp fringes of the Tethys Sea which covered the part of North Africa now known as the Sahara Desert.

Moeritherium stood about 0.6 m at the shoulder. It had no trunk but its teeth and skull reveal it was an early representative of a whole range of proboscids which later included ancestors of the present-day elephant and the tiny dassie or rock hyrax as it is known in East Africa.

Using fossil remains, scientists have identified five proboscid families, each of which tried to adapt to the circumstances that prevailed. Today only the family *Elephantidae* survives and two species of this — the imperial mammoth *(Mammuthus imperator)* and woolly mammoth *(Mammuthus primigenius)* — are also extinct.

The woolly mammoth survived until man established himself on earth. It had an undercoat of fine, soft, yellow to brown hair,

Dassie

Although the dassie was once at least three times its present 500 mm length, it is still hard to believe that this tiny creature is closely related to the elephant. In recognition of the relationship the restaurant at Sinamatella Camp is called The Elephant and Dassie.

The name, dassie, is commonly used in southern Africa. This word is Afrikaans deriving from the Dutch word *das* or badger. It is also sometimes called a rock rabbit. In East Africa they are known as hyrax which is scientifically more correct.

They are compact animals and an adult male in Hwange weighs about three kg. The centre back of the yellowspotted rock dassie, which occurs in Hwange, is yellow to ochre. The upper body hair is grizzled but soft with distinct white to off-white patches above the eyes. They are active in daytime in rocky areas where they warm themselves.

which was about 25 mm long, overlaid with a coat of long, coarse, dark rust-coloured hair some 500 mm long. They had very thick skin underlaid with fat, (which, with the hair, afforded protection against the rigours of the Northern Hemisphere climate), small ears 400 mm in length, and inwardly curving tusks.

Rock paintings in Europe depict groups of men trapping and stoning to death woolly elephants in pits, and whole frozen animals have been found in Siberia's permafrost. They are also recorded as having been on the menu at a banquet given by one of the Tsars in Leningrad.

Today there are two species of the family *Elephantidae*, the African elephant *(Loxodonta africana)*, and Asiatic elephant *(Elephas maximus)*. Both are highly intelligent and can be domesticated, the latter having been domesticated over 3,000 years ago.

Domestication of the elephant in Africa is a more modern phenomenon. In Zaire, forest elephants have been used to level an area for an aircraft landing strip, and in Botswana and Zimbabwe young bulls have been trained to provide rides for visitors. At Imire Ranch near Harare they are used for black rhino anti-poaching patrols and to pull ploughs and scotch carts.

The African elephant
The word elephant derives from the Greek word, *elephas,* which in Latin is *elephantus.* The word, pachyderms, often used in reference to elephants, refers to their thick skins.

The elephant is the most readily identifiable and unmistakable species of African mammals. It has a gnarled appearance like a well-weathered tree. The creased skin is thickest (30-40 mm) on the legs, forehead, trunk and back, and thinnest on the ears.

Very close up.

Sparse bristly hair covers the body, with juveniles, who grow up to the ages of 20 to 25 years, having more hair than adults. Adults have distinctive eyelashes and thick hair in the ears. The hair of the tail (1.5 metres long in the case of mature bulls) is in demand for bracelets and was once used as a pipe cleaner.

The colour of an elephant's skin is grey to brownish-grey although this can easily be disguised as a result of wallowing in mud or throwing dust or water over the body as a coolant and to control parasites.

The number of nails on an elephant's feet vary according to the terrain, some being torn off. Thick layers of cartilage in the feet act as

Trunks entwined.

shock-absorbers with the feet expanding and shrinking depending upon whether they are placed on the ground or raised.

The elephant's trunk fascinates. Raised horizontally with the tip probing the air like a radar antennae, it checks for danger. Its extraordinary dexterity is used in feeding, shovelling vast quantities of foliage into its mouth as it eats for about three-quarters of the day.

The ear flaps (*pinnae,* scientifically) are large, reaching a height of two metres in adult bulls. The ears, although weighing less than 20 kg each, constitute some 20 per cent of the body surface area and they have an extensive vascular system with a blood-flow rate of five to 12 litres per minute. They are vital to maintaining body temperature, emitting some three-quarters of the body's total heat loss.

Heat control through heat loss is of importance. One way is through the continual flapping of the ears. Others include the water intake (over 100 litres daily for more mature animals), cooling through swimming and wallowing, and tossing water and dust over the body. For the first two years after birth, mothers can be seen cooling their calves by throwing water and sand on them.

The elephant's eyes, green to hazel in colour, are relatively small without tear ducts and the mouth is small and spout-shaped.

A single pair of mammae or breasts are situated between the front legs of females and this is the only reliable way to distinguish post-puberty sexes although the shape of the female head tends to be more angular and convex than in males, which tend to be taller.

Elephants have temporal glands on both sides of the head, and a dark mark on the face behind the eye indicates secretion from these glands. This secretion can be copious when the animal is under stress or is excited.

The tusks are elongated upper incisor teeth and the tusk weight of elephants in southern Africa is much less than that of the East African elephant although the former is reputedly larger in body size, weighing up to six tonnes for older bulls and half that for cows. Female tusks are smaller than those of males and tuskless African elephants, genetically or through loss, are rare.

Wear and tear makes discrepancy between tusk sizes on a single animal the rule whilst the milk or first tusks are shed at about one year. Early on, the permanent tusks are capped with smooth enamel but this is swiftly lost with the entire tusk then comprising of ivory.

Accurate aging is difficult. Life expectancy in the wild is put at about 60 years. To a large extent, life expectancy is determined by the wearing down and breaking of the six successive sets of molars the elephant has, with animals declining physically when they can no longer properly masticate food because the last set of teeth has worn down.

Distribution
Before the arrival of Europeans and their firearms, elephants ranged freely throughout most of the sub-region, threatened only by the march of time, predators, and traditional hunting.

The Portuguese explorer, Vasco da Gama, reported the presence of elephants at Mossel Bay in the Cape Province of South Africa in 1497. Further inland in South Africa, a century and a half later, they were reported in large numbers. Today they only occur in South Africa in a few isolated and protected pockets.

European demand for ivory in the 17th century for piano keys, billiard balls, trinkets and ornaments — and the economic priorities of local white settler communities — was to change all this. In the space of 60 to 70 years to the turn of the 20th century, once abundant herds faced extinction.

In this period England alone imported 1.2 million lbs (roughly 550,000 kg) of ivory a year. To meet that demand by a single country some 50,000 elephants were killed. During the years of European demand for ivory, well over one million, and likely closer to two million, elephants were slaughtered.

Traders and settlers (known as *trekboers*) returned from the hinterland, wagons laden with ivory, from treks lasting up to nine months. One hunter reported having shot 22 elephants in a single day. The economic viability of early *Voortrekker* settlements in Transvaal were based almost exclusively on the ivory trade.

By 1858 the decimation of the elephant population in South Africa had reached such proportions that the Cape Colony published special legislation to try to protect them, and buffalo.

Having all but wiped out the elephant population in South Africa, the hunters moved north into present-day Mozambique and Zimbabwe. Of the 848,000 kg per year exported to Europe from 1879 to 1883 at the peak of the trade, only 29,000 kg originated in South Africa.

As late as 1875, elephants were reported to have existed in vast numbers in Zimbabwe. But a decade later few were reported to have survived. By 1900 the total Zimbabwe elephant population had fallen

Crossing the Hwange road.

below 4,000 and as late as 1930 the Hwange population was estimated to be a mere 1,000.

Prodded by the Governor of German East Africa (now mainland Tanzania), the European powers endeavoured to act in concert and, in London in 1900, after five years of deliberations, passed the *Convention for the Preservation of Wild Animals, Birds and Fish in Africa.*

This prohibited the hunting or killing of young elephants and introduced severe penalties, including confiscation of tusks weighing less than five kg. But the regulation became mired down in red tape and was easily circumvented by unscrupulous traders.

The value of ivory as an economic resource for the white settlers simply overrode the sentimental attitudes of the colonizers.

Zimbabwe's first game laws came into effect in 1902 and the Hwange National Park was created in 1932. Today, from the low of only 65 years ago — which is little more than the life of an elephant — Hwange's elephant population has increased to 30,000. That is certainly a tribute to the resilience of an animal once threatened with extinction and to the conservation methods of those who have protected the elephant.

Habitat and diet
African elephants are catholic in their habitat requirements. Their range is wide and diverse, from the arid stretches of the northern Namibian desert to the lusher woodlands, thick underbrush and heavy grass of Hwange.

Water, preferably fresh, is a further requirement as is shade in the hotter hours of the day. The Hwange elephants are highly mobile and can travel ten or more kilometres in a day in search of food and water.

Elephants are both grazers and browsers. A study in Hwange revealed that they fed on 87 browse species, 42 grass species and 36 herb species. The ratio between the types of food varies depending upon both availability and season with more grass eaten after good rainfalls. Mopane trees ranked high among the preferred browse species with elephants preferring to browse on previously damaged trees.

They are highly destructive animals as evidenced by the huge numbers of broken branches, flattened and barked trees to be seen throughout Hwange. Given their bulk, and their daily food requirement of around 170 kg (of which they digest only about 40 per cent) or six per cent of bodyweight, this is not surprising.

They have a disconcerting habit of flattening anything in their way. Larger trees are simply pushed over by extending their own trunk up the tree trunk, placing a tusk either side and simply pushing.

Pushing a tree.

With their trunks curled firmly around a supposed tasty morsel, they uproot whole bundles of grass, beating the clump against their legs or tusks to get rid of soil. Then the morsel is conveyed deep into the mouth by the trunk.

The trunk also plays a vital part in drinking. First water is inhaled into it. Then the trunk is lifted to the mouth into which the water is exhaled. To cool off they may squirt water over themselves. During droughts they will dig for water ("seep wells"), first using their feet and tusks, then the trunk.

They are second only to humans in their capacity to change their environment but, unlike our destructive capacity, elephants can also complement their environment.

Browsing on woody vegetation stimulates growth which can lead to an increase in primary production. Their dung, which is produced in quantities of well over 100 kg daily by adults, is the breeding ground and sanctuary for many species. The droppings of the Hwange herd have been estimated at well over one million tonnes a year and a single dropping has contained 1,925 acacia and 1,509 melon seeds.

Whilst it is not the intention here to be drawn into the unending argument as to whether or not elephants should be culled to protect their habitat and to maintain no more than the optimum population levels, the fact of the matter is the destruction they wreak on some species provides life for others.

Behaviour and social structure
Elephants are gregarious animals living in family groups consisting of an adult female (matriarch), her offspring and a number of closely related females with their offspring. On reaching puberty (about 12) young males within these groups leave of their own accord, joining other groups of young bulls, whilst the young females grow up and rear their calves within the family group.

The family groups can coalesce to form herds and the bulls join up with these herds, usually when a female is in *oestrus*, rejoining the male herd or remaining on their own as they grow older.

Bulls in *musth* actively seek out herds containing females in *oestrus*. *Musth* is a heightened sexual phase that bulls over the age of 30 experience annually. Where there is an absence of older bulls the restrained emotions of younger bulls may come into play.

This *musth* phase, which is hormonally determined, can last for up to three months against some six days for the female *oestrus*. The *oestrus* female selects a bull in *musth* to mate with on the basis of favourable genes.

While elephants do not display territorial attitudes, they do have home ranges which is the area they utilise for food and water. The optimum elephant density (which used to be referred to as carrying capacity) is put at 0.8 per square km. But, scientists admit, this figure is a generalisation as the optimum can vary according to vegetation type and water availability.

It is, therefore, a generalisation to extrapolate from the 0.8-per-square-km figure that the present 30,000 Hwange elephant population is too high and to propose an annual cull of 5,000.

The confidence level (CL) in the 1996 official figure of 22,762 elephants in Hwange National Park is 34 per cent, giving a swing from 18,712 to 26,812. Were the former figure to be accurate then the Hwange National Park population is almost exactly at its optimum elephant density level.

Elephants are normally extremely peaceful and in parts of Hwange, such as Hwange Estate where the Presidential herd mainly lives, they can be remarkably relaxed showing great curiosity and passing only inches from visitors in vehicles.

But it is important to remember they are wild animals. Staying in your vehicle is essential and great care must be taken not to get between a mother and her calf. Individuals, especially those which are sick or injured, can be very aggressive and dangerous.

It is as well to know the manifestations of threatening behaviour which can go even further. This can take the form of a raised head and trunk, extended ears, kicking up the dust, and screaming. Swaying or shaking the head may signal a mock charge. But mock charges can develop into the real thing with the trunk tucked below the jaw, trumpeting and screaming, tusks directed to impale the incautious.

A mock charge.

Above all, the ears express the mood. An angry elephant, ears extended, screaming and bearing down upon one, is a sight never forgotten.

Serious fights between males are rare although younger males indulge in playful, seemingly unending, sparring. The young, of either sex, behave very much like errant children with a mother's cuff occasionally needed to restore a modicum of discipline.

But elephants are deeply caring about each other. If one dies, is shot or darted (even for its own good to remove a snare), the others in the herd are likely to gather around to protect the inert mammal and will even try to carry away a body, wedging it between living animals.

Water remains one of Hwange's most serious problems. Elephants, in desperation, may drink brackish water which can kill them if the concentration of salts is too high. In Hwange elephants tend to gather at artificial waterholes where water is sodium rich.

43

Researchers have found that any decrease in the sodium content of the water leads to a corresponding decrease in the number of elephants drinking at a given waterhole.

Whenever elephants reach water, which in Hwange is daily, they will drink, bathe, spray themselves, and some may partially lie down. The elephant is completely at home in water and on Lake Kariba they can occasionally be seen swimming to islands with only their trunk above water like a submarine periscope.

From waterholes they will normally adjourn to a nearby mineral lick. The calves cavort and roll, young bulls spar, older ones look on sternly. Finally, with a low rumble, the matriach will indicate it is time to go. Slowly they move off, with the steady rolling walk of a tipsy sailor.

Reproduction
The peak period for conception is the rainy season — November to April in Hwange. The female *oestrus* lasts for about six days and during this time the female attracts bulls with a loud, low frequency call known as an *oestrus* rumble. The bulls may fight over a female but this is rare, as is the conception of twins.

Females carry their calves for roughly 22 months before giving birth which they prefer to do in a shady secluded retreat, preferably near water. The female may clear the ground in the area where she intends to give birth and frequently other cows and calves will surround the area, standing guard while the birth occurs.

The calf, on dropping free from the mother who will normally be in a squatting position to reduce the fall, severs the umbilical cord and the mother gently removes the membrane with her trunk and foot. The calf's first reaction thereafter is to search for the mammae and suckle.

At birth, calves measure about 900 mm at the shoulder. They are pinkish in colour and have more body hair than adults. Their eyesight is very poor and they maintain contact with their mothers by their trunks.

They normally wean after two years although some may continue suckling for up to three years. Young elephants, until their shoulder height is around 1.4 metres, are threatened by predators, particularly lion and hyena. They stick close to their mothers, walking between their legs under their bellies, and the herd will protect them vigorously if predators approach.

Mother and calf.

Maternal care is intense during the first two years. Mothers help young up and down slopes by gently pushing them with their trunks or forelegs, helping them over obstacles, and spraying them with water and sand to keep them cool.

The calves are extremely playful, squeaking and squealing with ears flapping as they barge into each other, bellowing loudly if hurt. It is this behaviour which, reminds one so much of human children.

OTHER HERBIVORES
Herbivore means a grass or plant-eating animal such as a cow, a horse, or many animals you will see in the wild including buffalo, zebra and wildebeest. They are characterised by having teeth adapted for grinding. Grass-eaters are called grazers, and plant-eaters are browsers.

Buffalo
Those familiar with the bush are probably more wary of this very large, heavily built animal than they are of any other. Adult males stand 1.4 m at the shoulder and weigh 800 kg. They move remarkably quickly, as anyone who has been chased can testify.

To support the massive body the legs are strong and stocky. The front hooves are larger than the hind to carry the huge head and neck. Older adult males are black, females a dark reddish-brown and juveniles distinctly reddish-brown.

45

Buffalo and Redbilled Oxpecker.

Their muzzles are short, hair-fringed ears large and hanging like domestic cattle, eyes ever watchful and baleful. Adult male horns can be massive atop a heavy boss with which they persistently pound victims.

You may well hear your guide refer to an aged male bull as "the old *daga* boy". It is because the buffalo wallows in mud *(daga)* and it indicates the respect those familiar with the bush have for these formidable and unpredictable adversaries.

In Hwange they occur throughout the park with the possible exception of the drier centre. They tend to be less visible to the visitor after the rains when they are more dispersed because of plentiful grass and water throughout the park.

But, as the extremities of the park begin to dry, herds of over 1,000 head for the artificial waterholes. In their wake they leave a dust cloud and their pace quickens as they near water.

Known as savannah buffalo (as distinct from the related, smaller horned, West African forest buffalo), their habitat must include plentiful grass, water and shade. They drink regularly, usually twice daily, graze and seek shade in the same area, and wallow as a means of controlling their temperatures.

Solitary bulls, who are particularly prone to predation by lions, may be seen in Hwange as well as bachelor groups of young and old bulls.

They are inquisitive as well as aggressive. They may advance, nose outstretched, to examine a vehicle. Disturbed, they race to rejoin the herd which is quick to stampede in all directions. Wounded, they are highly dangerous, sometimes circling and charging the unwary hunter from close range in thick bush.

The rinderpest epidemic in the last century all but wiped out the buffalo. In 1930 there were estimated to be as few as 100 in Hwange. Today there are several thousand. But, as carriers of foot-and-mouth disease, attempts are underway to isolate the buffalo from domestic cattle.

Rhinoceros — White and Black
Today the numbers of these two extinction-threatened species is officially a secret in Hwange. After the poachers' onslaught in the late 1980s and early 1990s, and the attendant media coverage, it was decided publicity attracted poachers. The best one can get from tight-lipped parks officials is that the rhino are "maintaining themselves".

One sympathises with this secrecy. De-horning the rhino, stepped-up anti-poaching patrols with a shoot-to-kill policy, aerial patrols and all manner of methods were tried to save the remaining rhino.

Whilst these met with some success, it was found that poachers who had tracked a de-horned rhino shot it anyway so they would not waste their time tracking a hornless animal next time.

Today most of the surviving rhino are closely guarded. In Hwange the black rhino exist in a fairly limited area near Sinamatella under continuous, and armed, army and parks guard. White rhino survivors can probably be counted on two hands.

But, unless the demand ceases by the end-users for rhino horns for their supposed medicinal properties, these species, which traces their ancestry back some 20 million years, faces little future in the wild.

Colour may not distinguish the white and black rhino, particularly if they have been wallowing or in dust. The colour of both is grey anyway. What will distinguish them, however, is the square lip of the white rhino as opposed to the hooked lip of the black rhino.

The white rhino is the larger of the two species with an adult male's shoulder height being 1.8 m and its weight over two tonnes. It is Africa's second largest land mammal behind the elephant.

The horns are composed of a mass of tubular filaments similar in substance to hair and are not bone at all as many suppose. While the white rhino is a grazer, the black rhino is a browser. The calves of both weigh about 40 kg at birth and the gestation period is around 15 months.

Hippotamus

Hippo probably account for more deaths than any other single mammal in Africa. Females with young can be particularly aggressive and there have been many reports of small boats being overturned and occupants killed.

But the very few hippo the Hwange visitor might encounter are most unlikely to be aggressive unless (this is rare in daylight hours) you get between the hippo and water they are making for.

Their name derives from a Greek word meaning water or river horse. Adults can remain under water for around six minutes, filling their lungs with air before submerging. Muscles close the nostrils and ears to prevent water entering. Their return to the surface is noisy as they empty their lungs with a loud blast.

Hippo.

They are not able to float, but they walk under water, usually along well-defined trails. In deep water they push themselves to the surface using their hind legs.

They are the only truly amphibious hoofed animals, feeding nocturnally on dry land and spending most of the day in the water where both mating and calving occurs. They eat 40 kg of grass nightly and may forage long distances for food.

The nostrils, ears and eyes are high on their heads allowing them to keep their heads above water to sense danger.

A large hippo weighs between one and two tonnes and the animal is unmistakable with its barrel-like body, short, stocky legs and very large broad face. The skin is greyish-black and the hippo's deep grunts and snorts are a notable African aquatic sound.

Fights between bulls can be fatal as they tear at each other with their formidable lower canines and defeated, scarred bulls retreat ignominiously. They are notable crop raiders which has led to control measures, and their meat and fat are prized for cooking purposes.

Giraffe

The tallest animal in the world, with the height of adult males being some five metres, their specific name, *camelopardalis,* means in Arabic, as big a camel and spotted like a leopard. They weigh over 1 tonne.

Hwange has around 2,000 giraffe which can be seen throughout the park, including regularly on what is known as the "ten-mile drive" looping from Main Camp via Nyamandhlovu Pan and back to the exit.

Giraffe necking.

Unmistakable among wildlife, the giraffe is covered in large, irregular-shaped darker markings which stand out in contrast to the off-white or yellowish background. These markings tend to grow darker with age.

Two conspicuous knob-like horns covered with black hair sit on top of the head at the end of the long neck. The lips are somewhat pinched allowing them to browse selectively on the leaves of thorn trees without eating the thorns.

They are mainly diurnal, resting in the shade during the heat of the day, either in a standing position or sitting down with their necks extended. They drink standing, splaying their front feet to allow their mouths to reach the water.

They walk and gallop in an unusual way. When walking the two legs on one side swing almost simultaneously and their gallop is ungainly. Even so, they have been timed at 56 km/h.

Unlike other species they cannot scratch an ear with a hind hoof and rely upon rubbing against trees to remove irritating ticks. Their hearing and sight are keen but there is disagreement as to their sense of smell.

They are generally docile animals but will vigorously defend their young against four-legged predators such as lions. Sparring occurs between males but, unlike with other species, rarely results in serious damage.

Courtship takes the form of literally necking, gestation lasts a little over a year, and calves are born with the mother standing in a bent position to lessen the drop, the umbilical cord breaking as the newborn falls to the ground.

Zebra
While the markings of no two zebra are alike, this is one of the easiest of Hwange's species to identify. They occur throughout the area, being seen most frequently in open grassland and woodland where they graze.

Their distinctive black and white markings may have shadow stripes underneath depending upon the sub-species. They are stockily built with forward protruding ears, a mane, and they have the overall look of a stocky work pony.

They live in family groups consisting of a stallion, one or more mares, and foals. Surplus stallions rejected by the group form bachelor herds.

They are timid and shy animals, particularly when approaching water, where they can be seen deferring to other species. Larger predators prey upon zebras with adult zebras vigorously defending their foals by kicking and biting. Under stress they bark (kwa-ha-ha) excitedly.

Zebra.

Female zebras and donkey stallions once mated freely and such semi-domesticated hybrids were used in the early white settler days to pull Zeederberg coaches from South Africa. The hybrids, which were known as Zebdonks, retained some of the pure zebra's markings, and were employed in tandem with pure donkeys in the 1950s to pull a milk cart in Bulawayo.

Warthog
This is one of the most captivating and busiest mammals to be found in the bush. They are predominantly grazers (grass-eaters), frequentally kneeling when feeding, and they run with their black tufted tails held erect.

Warthog.

Those less attracted to warthogs than this author have variously described them as "incarnations of hideous dreams" and "the most astonishing objects that

51

have ever disgraced nature". Such views fail to give this extraordinary animal its due credit.

They are widespread in Hwange and, although never counted, probably number several thousand. Most commonly they will be found in open grass or woodland and they are most active during the day.

The mud they have wallowed in may distort their normal greyish colour. The snout is pig-like, head elongated, the canine teeth develop into long curved tusks (sometimes used as beer mug handles), and the shaggy mane on the back is raised when the animal is stressed.

Boars have warts (in reality skin growths and not pure warts) behind the eyes and above the tusks while on the female there are only warts behind the eyes. Their legs are short and slender for their body mass with an adult male weighing 100 kg.

They live in disused burrows developed by other species adapting them to their needs. These burrows protect them against the climate and predators, their greatest enemy. Piglets enter the hole nose first, adults backwards, even when pursued, in a cloud of dust.

They occur in family groups, also known as "sounders", usually comprising of an adult male, female and offspring. Temporary bachelor groups also exist. They are generally sociable, with piglets normally born in the burrows early in the rainy season.

Aardvark
This mammal resembles no other, looking rather like a pinkish, long-snouted, cartoon pig with outsize ears and a kangaroo tail. It is appropriate that its name is derived from the Afrikaans words for earth-pig.

The aardvark is the only survivor of a now extinct mammal order. It is almost entirely nocturnal and rarely seen. Its diet consists of ants and termites and it favours overgrazed well-trodden areas where it finds it easier to locate its food. Aardvarks and baboons are omnivores which eat both animal and vegetable matter.

Baboons
There are two sub-species of baboon in southern Africa, Chacma and Olive. In Hwange you will only see the Chacma in troops numbering up to 100, usually in open country near water, and hear their bark.

The colour of individuals in a troop varies widely depending upon age, sex and geographical area. Generally they are light grey to dark grey-brown, have dog-like heads, brooding brown eyes and sit on their haunches.

Adult males will assiduously avoid eye contact — which makes them feel threatened — with humans, turning sideways or totally away. Females carry their young, who are extremely playful, slung under their bellies.

Baboon.

In Hwange, particularly around areas of human habitation such as Hwange Safari Lodge, you will also encounter vervet monkeys with their black faces and much lighter colour and weight. Keep your car and room locked as they — and baboons — are chronic thieves.

CARNIVORES
Twenty-seven carnivores — those who feed on other animals — from the King of the Jungle, the lion, to the mongoose, have been identified in Hwange. They are members of six families of the *Carnivora* order.

With the average visitor spending only three days in Hwange it is most improbable that you will see all of them.

Therefore, through pictures or descriptions, this Guide seeks to make it easier for you to identify those you may see. If you are with a guide he/she should be able to identify a given carnivore with which you may be unfamiliar.

If you are not with a guide, try to remember what the animal you see looks like so you can identify it later. Lion, leopard, cheetah and painted hunting dogs should be easy.

But you may have trouble distinguishing between other animals such as the seven species of mongoose found in Hwange. Try to remember the habitat where you see an animal, look for distinctive markings, visually measure the size and recall any other detail which might separate one from another. If possible make notes of what you have seen with the location, date and time.

If you are with someone else discuss what you have seen. Two people rarely see the same thing, traffic accidents being a classic case in point. So compare notes, try to create an agreed profile, and at the first opportunity try to identify what you have seen from a picture.

Lion
Africa's largest carnivore, the lion, tops virtually all visitors' lists as the animal they most want to see on their African safari.

Although nominally the King of the Jungle, few if any other species have had their range as dramatically reduced as the lion. Once they occurred widely in Europe, throughout much of Asia, and across the African continent.

The last remaining lions in Europe were killed in Greece around AD 100 and they were exterminated from Palestine about the 12th century. In Asia the few survivors occur in the Gir Peninsula in northern India.

In Africa, too, their range has been severely curtailed. They are now extinct in North Africa having disappeared from Tunisia and Algeria around 1891 and from Morocco in 1920.

In sub-Saharan Africa, where the largest concentration of lions survives today, their range has gradually been reduced as humans have expanded their own. Once they were common in South Africa's Cape Province. Today, outside zoos and reserves, they have vanished.

Very occasionally, lions, who are notable wanderers and opportunists, turn up in areas such as Windhoek, capital of Namibia, and on Zimababwe's central plateau or its eastern districts. But these are transitory migrants, often driven from drought areas in search of water and game which has moved ahead of them.

Lions are predominantly nocturnal and it is at night that they do most of their hunting and moving. In Hwange their roaring may be heard, although one must try to differentiate between the sound they make and that of an ostrich which is remarkably similar in one's befuddled state between deep sleep and total consciousness.

They are lethargic animals showing an aversion to exerting themselves except when intent on a kill. Even then they are highly inefficient with their kill ratio being much lower than that for hyenas or painted dogs. Buffalo herds frequently bear the morning-after scars showing where lions have hit and missed.

Usually the visitor will find lions lolling about or asleep in the shade, usually in prides, sometimes in small all-male groups. But, despite their apparent passivity, they can swiftly become aggressive if unduly disturbed, wounded or otherwise threatened.

Unlike most other carnivores they are distinctly social animals living and hunting in prides which can number a dozen or more and which may embrace several generations.

Prides tend to be found in areas where there is abundant game, frequently buffalo, zebra and wildebeest. The lioness is the nucleus of the pride although there may also be a dominant male. Fights between rival males for a pride may result in the death of one of the combatants.

Male lions become sexually mature at about two years old but usually have to wait another three years before mating. Females become pregnant for the first time at around the age of four and will produce litters every two years until they are around 15.

Lionesses.

The act of copulation between lions is notable for its foreplay and frequency. Courtship is initiated by either sex with the pair remaining closely together and the male following the female at all times and resting beside her.

Copulation occurs about every 15 minutes, lasting around a minute, over a period of several hours. During breaks the lion and lioness will lie beside each other or walk short distances before the next mating session.

The male may gently stroke the female on the shoulder, neck or back with his tongue to encourage submissiveness; he may seize her by the scruff of the neck (a painless largely symbolic act) during copulation, and the lioness can be heard purring.

Fertility from all this protracted effort is low and the number of cubs an impregnated female produces averages only 2.6. Cubs suckle for six to seven months and have a very high mortality rate — as high as 60 per cent in some recorded areas — due to scarcity of food, abandonment, disease and other predators.

An adult male lion's average weight is around 190 kg with females averaging 126 kg. Adult males, who stand 1.25 m at the shoulder, reach their maximum weight in seven years, females in five or six years.

The colour of adults is sandy or tawny on the upper body and white underneath. The backs of the rounded ears are black in stark contrast to the body colour. The tail, roughly half the length of the combined head and body, can be black tipped.

Adult males have a mane up to 160 mm in length which, with advanced years, can be black. The mane of younger males tends to be sandy or tawny although, in common with many species, climatic variations can affect colouring. Maneless male lions are rare.

Lions have five digits (toes) on the front feet and four on the rear. Each toe is equipped with very sharp, scimitar-shaped, retractable claws. Those claws, and the formidable lower jaw, are the main killing weapons.

Male lions rarely participate in the hunt, leaving this to the lionesses. But once a kill is made they take first priority with the lionesses having to wait until the male has eaten his fill.

Various means are employed to kill. Smaller game can be stunned with a blow from a paw, medium and larger game strangled. Warthogs can be dug out of their holes and in some cases victims have been killed through breaking their backs.

Nothing feels safe with lions around. Lions may kill baby elephants with the elephant herds reacting strongly to their presence. Other smaller animals — even mice and larger birds such as ostrich — are forced to be ever alert, to run at the least hint of danger.

Leopard
No two leopards, either in markings or colour, are alike. But, as you are likely to see very few if any of these powerful, secretive and largely nocturnal animals, you are unlikely to notice the differences.

Generally, however, they have black spots on the limbs, flanks, hindquarters and head, with irregular broken circles covering the remainder of the body.

They are Africa's largest spotted cats with an average male weighing 60 kg and a female a little over half that amount. In common with other cats they have five digits (toes) on the front feet and four in the rear and their spoor is more compact and circular than a lion's.

Leopard.

Leopards' ears are small and rounded, white whiskers particularly long, and their eyesight and hearing extremely keen enabling them to avoid obstacles in the dark.

Unlike lions they are solitary animals except during mating and post-birth periods. They are much more efficient and painstaking hunters, and they have withstood human encroachment much better with their range encompassing almost all of sub-Saharan Afica, the Middle and Far East, and Siberia.

Very rarely, they may be seen moving around in Hwange during the day. More commonly they lie up during the hotter hours in dense cover, the shade of rocks or caves, making them difficult to see. They may be heard making a hoarse rasping coughing sound, growling when under stress or threatened, and purring after food.

The best opportunity the visitor is likely to have of seeing this magnificent and elegant cat is when it is spread-eagled on a fairly flat branch where sometimes it will drag its overnight kill to avoid non-climbing predators.

Their prey tends to weigh no more than their own body weight, usually being killed after a relatively short chase. Impala and warthog are the preferred victims although different leopards appear to have dietary preferences and have been known to eat fish, reptiles and birds, which they pluck before eating.

Leopards tend to move at a slow, almost casual pace. But when disturbed they instantly switch to a bouncing gallop which, when they no longer feel threatened, gives way to a fast trot.

Whilst cheetahs chase down their prey, leopards, body crouched close to the ground, stalk their quarry before pouncing.

Cheetah
These svelte, graceful animals, built like greyhounds but physically resembling leopards, although with more distinctive spots and longer legs, are rarely seen in Hwange, preferring shorter, open grass savanah country and light bushland.

They are the fastest animals on earth, reaching speeds of over 100 km/h over short distances. Only one species of cheetah exists in southern Africa and they are genetically uniform making them highly susceptible to diseases.

Cheetahs' bodies, unlike those of the stockier more powerful leopard, are slender and held high off the ground on long thin legs. Their heads are much more rounded, muzzles shorter and ears smaller.

Cheetah.

The colonisation of Africa, demand for their skins, over-emphasis on their predatory impact on domestic stock and, less frequently, the demand for them as pets, has led to the shrinkage of their range and their disappearance in many parts of Africa.

They became extinct in India by 1952 and they have disappeared from countries they once inhabited bordering on the eastern Mediterranean. But they may still be found in northern parts of the Arabian Peninsula, Iraq, Iran, Afghanistan and Baluchistan.

Namibia claims to have the African continent's largest cheetah population and attempts are being made to re-introduce them in the Kariba area in Zimbabwe from which they disappeared when the lake filled.

They do most of their hunting in daytime, mainly around sunrise and sunset and, in common with lions and leopards, often lie-up in the hotter hours of the day on an elevated site warming themselves.

Cubs remain with their mothers for about a year, dispersing before another litter is born and males may form cohesive bachelor groups. They have very large, sometimes overlapping, home ranges which can cover hundreds of square km.

Unlike leopards, they are averse to swimming and are infrequent tree climbers. Their call is bird-like resembling a chirrup when excited and they may purr, growl, snarl, hiss or cough depending upon whether they are content or feel threatened.

They prefer to attack stragglers in prey groups, approach their intended victim openly, pausing only if it shows signs of nervousness, and then running the victim down with a short burst of no more than 400 m.

Hyena, Brown and Spotted

Both these species of hyena occur in Hwange but the third, the Striped Hyena, only occurs from northern Tanzania, into North Africa, through the Middle East, and on to India.

The dark brown coat of the brown hyena makes it easily distinguishable from the mottled markings of the spotted hyena. They are also indentified apart by the more rounded ears of the spotted hyena as opposed to the pointed ears of the brown hyena, and the shorter, less shaggy coat of the former.

Hyenas, until the Seventies, were believed to be scavengers lurking around the outskirts of the kills of other predators waiting to appropriate a morsel. Often they were exterminated as vermin.

But research on the spotted hyena has shown that whilst, in common with most predators, they do scavenge, they are most efficient and regimented hunters. And, despite their forbidding features, they can be tamed and will become very affectionate.

The hyena is readily distinguishable from other species by its heavy forequarters and sloping back. Their senses are highly developed and their night vision is particularly good, making hunting easier.

In Hwange you are more likely to see the spotted hyena which feeds on large-to-medium-sized hoofed animals such as young giraffe, zebra, wildebeest and antelope.

Their method of killing is to slow up their prey by biting until the rest of the pack catches up and brings down the victim. Unlike lions, female hyenas feed first on a kill and this, and the resulting larger meat intake, may explain why female hyenas tend to be heavier than males.

The somewhat chilling, long drawn out whoops of the hyena, which may be heard several kilometres away, is one of the highlights of the African night. Their giggling or laughter is another characteristic.

Painted Hunting Dog

A well-known saying holds: give a dog a bad name — and it sticks. Such has been the fate of *Lycaon pictus*, the African painted hunting dog.

There are few more beautiful, efficient and caring species in Africa. But, largely as a result of ignorance and disinformation, the hunting dog which once existed throughout Africa is today a severely threatened species.

They have been mercilessly persecuted, misunderstood, maligned and slaughtered. They have been shot on farms, even in national parks, and continually run over by speeding motorists. Between 1956 and 1961 a total of 2,674 were shot in Southern Rhodesia, condemned to death as vermin.

In Southern Rhodesia their population was reduced to probably less than 100 and it is a miracle this unique evolutionay line survived at all. Today the total population on the whole continent is between 2,000 and 3,000 and most of these are in unsafe or prey-depleted areas.

Painted Dogs.

Zimbabwe today has some 700 survivors and is one of the only four countries with a known population stronghold. Many of the survivors exist in Hwange National Park and surrounds where special dog crossing signs have been erected on main roads to try to curtail the numbers killed by vehicles.

Gregory Rasmussen, known to Hwange guides as "Mr Dog", heads the Painted Dog Research Project. He cares passionately about the dogs and he can frequently be seen in the area holding aloft a radio mast and wearing earphones as he tries to locate and track Hwange's collared dogs and those on adjoining farmlands.

In large measure his research role has given way to the post of conservationist, publicist and custodian of the surviving dogs. He lectures at schools, to wildlife groups, to farmers — or anyone else prepared to give him a hearing — trying to change attitudes.

The Hwange road signs, the only ones of their kind in the world, are his brainchild. So are the illuminated collars to easily identify known packs and the studs on the collars making it easier for a trapped dog to break out of a snare.

His enthusiasm is contagious. Stockily built and black-bearded, he continually elicits support for the threatened dogs from diverse donors.

The painted hunting dog first appears in fossil records some 15 million years ago. It is not related to the domestic dog and while (particularly after hunting and feeding) it is extremely docile, it has never been domesticated. Equally there is no record of it ever attacking humans.

The dog is a predator and in Zimbabwe aproximately 98 per cent of their diet comprises of impala, kudu and duiker. They are extremely efficient hunters, killing their prey in seconds.

The home range of packs is enormous, some 750 square km. They are capable of top speeds of 70 km/h, trot at 15 km/h and with ease they travel 20 to 30 km daily.

They are deeply caring carnivores when it comes to their pups. Only one pair breeds annually within a pack and the whole pack participates in feeding, protecting and rearing the young. And, unlike other predators such as lions, the pups eat first on a kill.

A pack (you will rarely see them alone) of painted hunting dogs in the wild is a privileged and unforgettable sight. Their mottled (each dog is different) dark brown, yellow and white markings and rounded ears make it impossible to believe that anyone could regard this beautiful creature as vermin.

Aardwolf

The aardwolf, which looks like a smaller version of a hyena, is mainly a nocturnal animal which you are unlikely to see except on night drives.

Like the hyena it is higher on the shoulders — accenuated by a hairy dark mane which stands on end when the animal is stressed — than on the hindquarters. Its body colour is usually pale buff with the body encircled by distinctive black hoops. The muzzle, tip of the tail and feet are black.

They are solitary foragers, with termites making up the bulk of their diet, and they live in dens.

The aardwolf is normally silent only being heard under stress when it may emit a soft clucking sound or, if captured or seriously threatened, a deep-throated growl. They are territorial animals marking the extremities of their domain.

Although its canine teeth are well developed, there is no evidence to support the claim that they kill sheep.

Caracal
This powerfully built cat with its long ears, black interspersed with white, is often erroneously referred to as a lynx. Its hindquarters are slightly higher than the shoulders and its body is reddish in colour with paler underparts.

Caracals occur throughout much of Africa as well as in the Middle East, Afghanistan, Pakistan and India. They have been deemed to be a problem animal and killed as vermin.

Whilst they are commonly found in open grasslands, particularly vleis, and lightly wooded areas, they can tolerate semi-desert conditions.

Solitary, secretive, and predominantly nocturnal, caracals kill medium and smaller prey, including young antelopes, birds and the smaller mammals such as mongooses, hares and rabbits.

African Wild Cat
While the African Wild Cat's body colours vary from pale tawny to grey, depending upon the species and whether the habitat is dry or wet, it is best likened to a large domestic tabby.

They do breed with domestic cats. But the African Wild Cat can be seperately identified by the rich red colour behind its ears and the long front legs which raise the body when sitting to a near vertical position which the domestic cat cannot emulate.

The African Wild Cat occurs widely on the continent except in tropical or montane forest areas. They are predominantly nocturnal mainly eating birds, lizards, mice and rats.

Serval

This elegant carnivore looks somewhat like a miniature cheetah. It has a long neck and legs, large pointed ears accentuating its small head, a spotted coat and white underbelly.

Servals exist widely south of the Sahara as well as in Morocco and Tunisia. They are restricted in their habitat by water availability and occur more commonly where there is permanent water and/or high rainfall.

In common with many cats they are primarily nocturnal and may be seen in vehicle headlights. Their preferred prey are mice or rats followed by birds and reptiles.

Civet

Frequently called the civet cat this animal is in fact related to the mongoose or ferret common in Europe and is only very distantly related to the cat.

Individual civets vary enormously in colour and no two are exactly alike. But a combination of black, grey and white patterns are common to all of them.

Civets walk with an arched back and a ridge of dark hair on the spine is raised when they feel threatened. They prefer to live in woodlands near water, are found singly or in pairs, have a fixed home range and eat a wide range of food including insects, wild fruit, mice, reptiles and birds.

Genet, Large-spotted and Small-spotted

Small-spotted Genets are common in Hwange, most likely to be seen in the broken country at Sinamatella or around Main Camp, while Large-spotted Genets are more frequent in the northern part of the park from Shumba to Bumbusi.

Markings vary on both species. They have long sleek bodies, foxy faces, long bushy tails, and distinctive black spots. The Large-spotted Genet is rusty-brown in colour with a black-tipped tail, while the Small-spotted Genet is greyish to off-white with a white tip to its tail.

The Large-spotted Genet is more frequently found in fairly dense vegetation with water nearby while the Small-spotted Genet has a more varied habitat, including rock outcrops. Both are equally at home in trees, are nocturnal, and eat rodents, birds and reptiles.

Jackel, Side-striped and Black-backed

As the names of these two species suggest, it is easy to differentiate between them. Both look foxlike and will most frequentally be seen singly or in pairs.

Side-striped Jackal have a greyish colouring with a light, black-fringed, band along each flank. Their bushy tails are mainly black with a white tip. Apart from the black saddle, the Black-backed Jackal is greyish to reddish-brown in colour. The tail is mainly black.

Black-backed Jackel.

The Black-backed Jackal, often seen in the wings at other predators' kills, will eat almost anything, including carrion. Their call is a screaming yell ending with a few dog-like yaps. The Side-striped Jackal is quieter, more secretive, usually solitary, found near water, and somewhat more selective about its diet.

Bat-eared Fox

Resembling small jackals they are easily identifiable by their disproportionately large rounded ears, pointed, frowning muzzles, black tail and legs.

They occur in two regions of Africa only, East and Southern, which are separated by some 1,200 km. These two population strongholds were probably connected during the Pleistocene era which was drier.

In Hwange they occur widely in the northern part of the park but may be seen near Main Camp. They prefer basalt soil areas, usually live in burrows, and feed on termites, reptiles, rodents and fruit.

Honey Badger

Immortalised by the late Ernest Hemingway, this powerfully built, short-legged carnivore with very small eyes, is unmistakeable as it moves at a lumbering trot, nose close to the ground, scenting its prey. It has a broad, light-coloured saddle running from the neck to tail in contrast to its jet black underparts and limbs. Its short, stumpy tail is unusually erect when it runs.

They occur widely in most mopane areas in Hwange but are rarely seen. Their thick skin protects them from stings when they raid bee-hives and they also eat scorpions, reptiles and birds. They fear no enemies and have been known to fight a lion.

Mongoose
Seven sub-species of mongoose have been recorded in Hwange. Of these you are most likely to see two — the Banded Mongoose and the Dwarf Mongoose — which occur widely throughout the park.

Banded Mongoose live in large groups numbering over 30 and may readily be seen around Hwange Safari Lodge and Main Camp. They shelter in termite mounds and other nearby bolt-holes, cheeping continuously, and nervously watching the sky for hawks.

Dwarf Mongoose, which are dark brown in colour, move in smaller groups. Each group is dominated by a male and female and they are usually found in open or rocky areas.

ANTELOPE
Eighteen species of antelope have been recorded in Hwange National Park. Some, such as the magnificent sable and delicate impala, are common. So too are the tiny Common Duiker (if you have sharp eyes), Wildebeest, Kudu and Waterbuck.

Other antelope such as the Roan, Red Hartebeest, Bushbuck, Reed-buck, Klipspringer, Steenbok, Sharpe's Grysbok, Gemsbok and Oribi are uncommon and will only be seen with luck and in specific areas. Tsessebe, the fastest antelope, may be seen in the Dete vlei and occasional Eland herds in open grasslands.

Sable
With their sweeping scimitar horns, black-satin sheened bodies (in the case of adult males), pure white hair beginning on the muzzle and extending along the belly ending under the tail, this is one of Hwange's most photogenic animals.

They exist throughout most of the park although they are more frequently found in open mopane woodland in the vicinity of water. While predominantly grazers they are also known to browse.

An adult bull weighs around 230 kg. While the bulk of his coat, including the vertical standing mane, will be black, younger males, females and juveniles tend to be reddish-brown.

It is possible to judge, but not pinpoint, age from the sweep of the horns which are longer for males than females. Heavily ringed in front for most of their length, the longest horns recorded in the region were 1.47 m.

Sable adults, juveniles and calf.

They are gregarious animals existing in herds of 30 or more in Hwange. Their social structure includes territorial bulls, nursery herds and bachelor groups.

Territorial bulls, through intimidation or actual fighting, defend their territories vigorously. In serious fights the bulls drop to their knees and slash at each other with their lethal horns which can result in serious injuries or death.

Nursery herds can be quite large, with males evicted at about the age of three by the dominant bull, after which they join bachelor groups awaiting their turn to become dominant.

The nursery herds normally have a dominant female concerned primarily with welfare. They determine the herd's movements, lead the way to water or feeding, keep watch for danger and direct the herd's flight.

In all but the sexual act and its foreplay, the female remains subservient. But, during the foreplay, the male will approach and scent her. If the scent is promising he will raise his head and draw back his lips exposing his gums and teeth.

Then he will approach the female gently tapping her hindlegs with his foreleg. If she responds by standing still the act of consummation follows. If she moves off his overtures have been premature.

Impala
This is the most commonly seen antelope in Hwange. It is also the most graceful of the antelopes with a shiny reddish-fawn uppercoat, paler sides and white chest, belly, throat and chin.

Impala.

Its legs are long and slender and both buttocks have a vertical black stripe. Only the males have harp-shaped horns sweeping back from their heads before bowing and ending in sharp points.

Their preferred habitat is lightly wooded grassland with water nearby. They are to be found in herds which increase in size to 100 or more during the wet season and early dry season. Males are only territorial during rutting with the normal social structure being confined to breeding and bachelor herds.

Impala both graze and browse depending upon the season and food availability. Because they perpetually scavenge for food during daylight hours they have been given their demeaning nickname — the "goats of the bush" — which belies their grace, particularly their bounds when alarmed or playing.

Mating is in Zimbabwe's autumn and is influenced by the lunar cycle occurring during full moon. The lambs are born during November to January after a gestation period of roughly 200 days.

Duiker
These tiny antelope earned their name from the Afrikaans word *duik* meaning "dive", on account of the way they duck and dive in a series of plunging jumps when disturbed.

They are small, easily hiding in tall grass. Grey-brown to reddish-yellow in colour with white insides on their underparts, limbs, inside the tail and ears, and dark brown to black on the facial blaze and forelegs, they are easily identifiable when still.

Females, weighing about 20 kg, are heavier than males but only the males carry short straight, heavily ridged, horns .

Whilst they occur in most vegetations except forest, they will hide in forests to escape detection. They are also absent in desert regions penetrating them only when following water courses with vegetation which provides shelter and shade.

They are normally solitary animals although they pair up during mating and females can be seen with their young. They will lie up at the approach of danger, jumping up at the last moment, literally at one's feet, and disappearing as swiftly with plunging jumps in a zig-zag course for the nearest cover.

Wildebeest

The music hall revue artists, Flanders and Swann, popularised this animal well beyond its habitat with their song "I'm a Gnu... how do you do?".

Apart from being called a gnu, the more correctly named blue wildebeest is locally known as "The Clown of the Plains" in recognition of its eccentric behaviour.

Its colour is silvery-grey sometimes tinged with brown which, in certain lights, gives it a bluish-grey hue. Vertical stripes are discernable on the body. Adult males stand 1.5 m at the humped shoulder and the lower hindquarters seem comparatively frail.

Wildebeest.

Their large, elongated heads, black bearded throats, broad horns, flowing manes and sweeping tails set them apart. They are grazers commonly seen with zebra and impala, or laying up in light shade in the heat of the day near water. Solitary males will be seen maintaining territory awaiting the arrival of females in the mating season.

Kudu

To many, this elegant animal ranks among the most handsome of the antelope species. It was once described as the "acme of Nature's efforts to attain perfection of type".

Adult males stand 1.4 m at the shoulder and weigh 250 kg. Their body colour is fawn-grey with up to 14 unevenly spaced vertical white stripes running down the sides of the body from the neck to the rump.

Facial markings vary enormously. But generally these tend to consist of a V-shaped white band beginning just below the eyes and ending part way down the nose which is darker than the body colour. The lips are edged with white hair.

Kudu.

Kudu's ears are distinct and rounded, the tail bushy and like a white powder puff on the often exposed underside, and the bull is adorned with large corkscrew horns which continue to grow throughout his life. From the number of spirals in the horns the age of the bearer can be fairly accurately assessed. Females and juveniles are a more cinnamon colour.

Kudu are a savannah woodland species preferring acacia and are not found in desert, forest or open grassland areas. They have proved remarkably resilient to hunting and settlement pressure and such sub-regional disappearance as has occurred, in common with many animals, has mainly been in South Africa.

Waterbuck

This large, stocky antelope with its shaggy grey-brown coat, is easily recognisable by the distinctive white circle on its rump. The most common explanation for this unique marking is that it is so placed for the animal behind to follow easily.

They also have a white collar around the throat, white markings below the eyes and around the nose, and the hair on the legs tends to be darker than that on the body.

Waterbuck.

Males stand 1.2 m at the shoulder and weigh over 250 kg. As the name suggests they are usually to be found near water in small to medium size breeding or bachelor herds.

Only males carry horns which rise from the top of the

head and sweep forward in a single curve. They are smooth at the tips and heavily ringed over the first three-quarters of the distance from the head.

They have a strong goat-like smell and can often be smelt before they are seen. They are territorial and the males adopt a "proud" posture with head and body erect, and the whites of their eyes prominently displayed, as a means of intimidating intruders. Should this fail serious fighting ensues with waterbuck tending to fight more than other ungulates.

Eland
This is the largest African antelope with fully grown males standing 1.7 m at the shoulder and weighing up to 700 kg. Females are smaller at 1.5 m and weigh about 450 kg.

Eland occur in the wild from Uganda southwards but in South Africa they are confined to the Kruger National Park and environs. They were once widespread in Zimbabwe but now only occur in the northwest, southeast and parts of the Eastern disctricts.

Colouration between the northern and southern eland in the sub-region varies with Zimbabwe being a meeting place. They are generally dun-coloured with older eland darker in colour because of hair loss with the skin colour showing through.

Adult bulls have a patch of dark, coarse hair on the forehead, a sort of mane down the back, and the lengthy tail ends in a pronounced tuft of black hair.

Both sexes have horns, males being heavier. The horns are distinctly spiralled over the first half of their straight rise from the head, readily distinguishing the eland from other antelope such as the Kudu.

Eland.

They are versatile in their habitat requirements being found in arid semi-desert and montane grassland areas. They are predominantly grazers, drinking regularly when water is available. In areas where water is not easily available they rely on moisture from their food.

While they generally occur in small groups, herds of over 700 have been recorded in Hwange National Park and elsewhere in the region. They are timid animals but are easily tamed and worked with domestic cattle. Gestation is approximately 270 days.

The largest known herd of eland, numbering several thousand, exists in the Ural Mountains of the USSR. They were introduced there by a former Tsar because of the lower butter-fat content of their milk and lack of cholesterol.

Bushbuck
This is a shy, medium-sized antelope. The Chobe Bushbuck is Bambi-like in appearance, with the rump appearing somewhat higher than the shoulders. Regional colour variation occurs.

Generally in Zimbabwe, they are a rich chestnut to dark fawn in colour with patterns of vertical white lines and spots on the flanks giving a highly distinctive look. The tail is bushy, dark brown above, white below, and only rams have horns.

Pairs of males are uncommon. They are selective browsers but will eat grass. In forestry areas and gardens they have been cited as a problem animal nipping off young buds.

Bushbuck.

BIRDS

With a bird list of some 420 species, Hwange National Park is a prime destination for bird watching. And, because of Hwange's diversity and size, a bird-watching safari needs to be carefully thought out and planned bearing in mind ecological variations and climatic vagaries.

Seasonal occurrence of species make the time of year important. Migrant seasons are the hot-wet months (November to April), cool-dry months (May to July), and hot-dry months (August to November). Some of these migrants arrive from within Africa, others from Europe.

Saddlebilled Stork.

Beyond that the visitor should bear in mind Hwange's three geological/ecological areas. These influence the number of species in a given area. On the boundary of the northern basalt area and the Kalahari sands there are extensive seasonal pans. These pans are an important habitat for birds and when rain-filled they are the site of rare and interesting species.

Occurrences are unpredictable in both space and time and entirely dependent upon when the pans fill, the water extent and geological area concerned. So even the best laid plans can fall victim to unpredictable vagaries.

In effect this means if the pans near Shumba are full and those at Main Camp are empty, birds are more likely to gather at the former. If the pans near Main Camp fill later it is likely viewing will not be as good there if the birds have first used suitable habitat elsewhere.

Marabou Stork.

The timing of the rains is also important. The optimum time for Hwange pans to fill and provide outstanding bird viewing, is January to March — provided other pans in the northwest of the country have not filled earlier. If all the elements combine obligingly then Hwange pans can provide a veritable feast of viewing, particularly of waterfowl.

The basalt areas to the south of the Kalahari sands become very water-logged during good rains and areas become impassable. There are some seasonal pans in this part of the park but as far as is known, partially due to inaccessibility, they do not support the same numbers and diversity of birds as those on the ecotone to the north.

The habitat in the south is mainly mopane woodland which limits the birds that may be seen in this area. Access to these areas is limited for normal tourist traffic, leased concessions being controlled by safari operators.

In contrast, the northern basalt area is quite accessible to self-drive tourists and the area contains a number of interesting species for birders. The vegetation changes as one moves east from the Botswana border through the seasonally flooded vleis at Robins Camp. Then come the stunted woodlands on the higher intervening ground, mixed deciduous woodland away from the grasslands on the high ground, and the acacia and other woodlands along some of the rivers which ultimately flow north into the Deka River.

Further east, there is a dam at Salt Pan which, because of the slightly saline water, is an excellent place for wading and other birds. Still further east the dams at Deteema and Mandavu are well worth a stop for birders.

The habitat turns increasingly to mopane interspersed with extensive riverine forest along the Sinamatella and Lukosi rivers as one proceeds further east. Before emptying into the Zambezi River further north, their riparian forest provides tongues of suitable habitat for interesting birds found nowhere else in Hwange.

The terrain between Deteema Dam and Sinamatella is quite rugged and extends into the Matobo-like granite formations between Tshakabike Spring, to the east of Sinamatella, and Mambanje, close to Dete, which is just outside the park's north-eastern boundary formed by the Bulawayo-Victoria Falls railway line. These rugged areas are a haven for birds of prey. Recently a Crowned Eagle was seen in this area and the only Hwange record of Black Eagle breeding also comes from this terrain.

Pied Kingfisher.

The Kalahari sand area, which dominates the park, contains a number of unique features mirrored in the birds which may be observed.

Overall, Hwange National Park forms an interesting transitional area with some western species reaching the outer edge of their range here, whilst some eastern species do not penetrate the drier sands to the west. Frequently these birds are similar.

The colourful Crimsonbreasted Shrike, occurs primarily in Kalahari sand areas and is absent in the basalt areas where its niche is filled by the Tropical Boubou which is on the western end of its range. Another example is the Kalahari Robin whose niche to the east and north of the Kalahari sand area is filled by the Whitebrowed Scrub Robin.

Crimsonbreasted Shrike.

75

Lilacbreasted Roller.

Hwange is of conservation importance for a number of birds in Zimbabwe and in a sub-continental context. The range of the Ostrich has been significantly reduced and Hwange holds Zimbabwe's only consequential wild population.

A substantial number of large raptors breed within Hwange and research has shown that their territory (and this includes vultures) is significantly smaller in basalt areas than in Kalahari sand areas. This is thought to be because basalt soils retain more moisture and nutrients than Kalahari sands and thus have greater productivity.

Recently a wing-tagged Lappetfaced Vulture was recorded in Hwange. This bird had been ringed as a nestling in South Africa's Kruger National Park some months earlier and the sighting highlights the importance of large protected areas, with their mammalian carnivores, to the conservation of large scavenging birds on the sub-continent — and probably beyond.

Similarly, Hwange forms a niche for important species such as the two oxpeckers frequently seen picking ticks and other insects from wildlife and domestic cattle. The current population of Yellowbilled Oxpeckers found in Matobo National Park derives from the Hwange National Park.

Hwange is one of the few protected areas in Zimbabwe which incorporates a significant number of seasonally flooded wetlands. These wetlands, or pans, are important sub-continental breeding areas for such species as Dwarf Bitterns and other water birds. They are also especially important for crakes, the ecotone area of Hwange National Park having the highest diversity of crakes in the country.

One special feature of Hwange which proposes a rainy season visit is the termite eruptions in that season and the numbers of migrant eagles and falcons feeding from these eruptions.

TREES and SHRUBS

The type of soil in a given area determines the flora one finds in Hwange where over 1,000 plant specimens, including 250 different trees and 200 grasses, have been identified.

And, as can be seen from the sections on mammals and birds, as well as those to come on reptiles and butterflies, it also determines the species one is most likely to see in a given area. Thus, this section on flora is broken down into the nine main vegetation types occurring in the park showing where you will most commonly find them.

South of the watershed (the southern and central sections of Hwange) on Kalahari sand one finds five main vegetation types. These are:

Baikiaea/Pterocarpus woodland and open woodland which exists in Kalahari sand areas and covers the bulk of the park. Grasses are varied and there are common perennial grasses in this area.

Burkea/Terminalia open woodland.

Acacia woodland, again on Kalahari sand, represented by woodland or open woodland. It is in these areas that one will find the highest level of elephant damage to trees.

Open grassland and *vleis*. Kalahari sand again underlays these areas to be found around Main Camp and Kennedy, and along drainage lines such as those around Linkwasha and Manga. Some of the vleis are loamy and in the Dete vlei combustion of peat can occur. Good areas for small mammals such as impala, zebra and wildebeest who like a clear view to watch for danger.

Scattered *Combretum* and open grassland. Such areas, associated with open grassy glades on Kalahari sand depressions, are similar to the area described above. But they are not on drainage lines. They are to be found on "Ten-mile drive", at Makwa and Ngweshla where the vegetation includes combretum and buffalo thorn.

North of the watershed (northern section) the underlying geological base is basalt. There are four main vegetation types. These are:

Colophospermum mopane woodland and open woodland. This is an area of shallow soil on basalt, sandstone and shale, with mopane the dominant feature. It is most commonly found in the Sinamatella and Robins areas where wildlife tends to be more seasonal and less easy to see. A large area of mopane woodland also occurs in the south of the park in the Zibanini/Leasha area on loamy-clay soils.

Open grassland occurs on heavy black soils in the Robins and Windmill areas.

Colophospermum mopane/Brachystegia will be found most commonly in broken hilly country around Tshakabika and Mtoa Ruins and between Masuma and the Shumba picnic site in mixed woodland.

Riverine vegetation will only be found along the park's rivers, the Lukozi and Deka being the main ones. Sausage and ebony trees may be found along the banks of these rivers.

Baobab trees

Baobab trees, accredited by legend of holding up the sky, can be found in many areas of Hwange National Park, particularly the more arid ones.

The elephantine trunks of these ungainly giants appear disproportionate to their scraggy upper branches.

But they are trees steeped in history, myth and belief. A person who drinks an infusion of the bark becomes mighty and strong, one who drinks water in which the baobab seeds have been soaked is protected against crocodiles.

The first recorded attempt at dating these trees was done in 1749 by a French botanist, Michel Adanson, who gave the botanical name, Adansonia digitata, to the tree. His calculation was that a tree (regarded as the oldest on earth) at the mouth of the Senegal River was 5,150 years old.

Recent carbon dating puts the age of some baobabs at over 3,000 years and certainly the baobab is the longest surviving tree known today. They have been used to sanctify burial grounds, as hiding places, in rain-making ceremonies, and so large are their girths it is said one can hollow the trunk and drive a carriage and horses through.

REPTILES

During a 1993/94 survey of Hwange National Park, a total of 104 species of reptiles — 45 snakes, five Chelonians (tortoises and terrapins), 30 lizards and 24 frogs — were identified.

The study was done by Gregory Rasmussen for Zimbabwe National Parks and Zimbabwe Natural History Museum, where he is a field associate.

Gregory is heavily into snakes and, to the consternation of fellow passengers on a train, once temporarily "lost" a black mamba look-alike, one of several snakes he was taking back to school.

Beadle

There is one other Hwange reptile who deserves special mention. Beadle is to be found in the waterhole overlooked by the viewing platform at Nyamandhlovu pan. The crocodile was presented to Hwange National Park by the former Southern Rhodesian Chief Justice, Sir Hugh Beadle, when it became too large for his suburban fishpond. For years it was named after him after it took up residence at Nyamandhlovu. Then "Sir Hugh" produced offspring and "his" name was swiftly changed to "Lady Beadle".

To those of nervous disposition, Gregory sounds positively blasé when he talks about Hwange's snakes. Only six of the 45 are potentially lethal — the Black Mamba, Western-snouted Cobra (it used to be known as Eygptian Cobra), Spitting Cobra, Puff Adder, Boomslang and the shy Vine Snake. he stresses.

Neither Boomslangs nor Vine Snakes have ever given anybody what he calls an "accidental bite", their victims always being handlers. And whilst the Spitting Cobra does just what its name says, blindness in the victim will only be temporary if the eye is swiftly washed with water or some other liquid. So that narrows the list!

Three other Hwange snakes, the Stiletto Snake, which looks like a blind worm and frequently bites unsuspecting people who pick it up, the Snouted Night Adder and the Rhombic Night Adder, can all give one a "nasty swelling" which is best cured by rest.

The other 36 Hwange snakes — in fact 80 per cent he stresses — are non-venomous. But, even for those who might be tempted to handle a snake, identifying one from the other, often in seconds, is hazardous and, on the very rare occasion that one sees a snake, they are best left alone and to experts. Most snakes only want to escape anyway.

The other reptiles in Hwange are much more approachable. Of the Chelonians, two of the species are tortoises and three are terrapins.

The two species of tortoise, Leopard and Speke's Hinged, are most commonly seen after the rains and are readily identifiable from their differing shell shapes and markings. Just look for leopard-like spots on the shell of one and a hinge on the rear part of the shell of the other.

Of the three species of terrapin, two of them, the Marsh Helmeted Terrapin and the Panhinged Terrapin, can be seen literally running, albeit at their own ponderous pace, from one waterhole to another during the rains seeking to colonise a new area. They may also be seen basking on the backs of resident hippos.

The lizards, some of them highly coloured such as the Agama with its bright blue head and brown body, can be most readily seen in the rocky Sinamatella area. The rainbow rock skink may also be seen, males having bright orange heads and females blue heads. The common chameleon is also widespread but a master of disguise most easily identified when it turns black when threatened.

Frogs are definitely fun, some tiny and beautifully coloured, others more toad-like. Their wonderful calls (or are they musical croaks?) can be heard during the rains and the most common one you will hear is the Senegal Running Frog, better known as the Champagne Frog because of the bottle-popping sound it makes.

You will also hear the Striped Pixie Frog, a rather nondescript toady-looking character who emits a sound resembling a rusty wheel turning. And in sandy areas you may encounter the Kalahari Toad which is most raucous, calling during the day when there is no rain about.

One character you are bound to meet during the rains is the Dung Beetle, some of whom have rhino-like horns jutting out in front of them, and who roll dung (frequently elephant which is larger and plentiful) into balls which they push away with their hind legs and then bury to lay their larvae in.

BUTTERFLIES

Resident butterfly enthusiast and guide at The Hide, Daryl Martyn, lists seven families of butterflies, and 116 species of their sub-families, the Hwange visitor may see.

The first is the *Dinainae* sub-family (milkweed butterflies) of the *Nympalidae* family with three species — the African Monarch, Layman and Chief — all occurring in Hwange. These tough-bodied, slow-flying butterflies have light-spotted, elongated abdomens and medium-sized wings.

The Monarch is the most common in Hwange. They are distasteful or unpalatable to predators because of their toxic content as a result of feeding almost exclusively on milkweeds. Their colours — red and orange — have been adapted over thousands of years and serve as a warning to predators. Other butterflies now copy these colours for protection.

There are 16 species of the *Acraenae acraeas* sub-family of the *Nymphalidae* family in Hwange. Like the Monarch, they are tough, hard to kill and distasteful containing hydrogen cyanide forcing the unsuspecting predator to rapidly release them. Their rubbery exoskeleton enables swift recovery from attack.

Brick-red, orange or carmine in colour, they are gregarious butterflies frequently found feeding in large numbers on flowers or in open grassland. They land with their wings open, which distinguishes them from several other species, and slowly open and close their wings after landing.

Five species of the *Satrinae* (evening browns) sub-family of *Nymphalidae* occur in Hwange. They are well-camouflaged, dull-coloured, slender in structure and have fairly weak flights. They are small, most frequently found in the shade in the undergrowth of low vegetation.

The final and most populous of the *Nymphalidae* family includes charaxes, nymphs and commodores. Readily attracted to bait traps, they are recognisable in flight by their rapid and powerful wing beats followed by a short glide. They are very alert and evasive, often found on stream banks, rotting fruit, gum from trees, even rotting meat and carnivore dung.

Swallowtails, the largest and most beautiful butterflies, are members of the *Papilionidae* family. Six species occur in Hwange. The most common is the Citrus Swallowtail, also known as the Christmas butterfly. It is regarded as something of a pest feeding on citrus trees and is generally brightly coloured with a pungent odour. They patrol their territories and, particularly on humid days, feed on flowers, near water.

The most common, medium-sized whites to be found in Hwange are from the *Pieridae* family. They are extremely alert, vigorous fliers, and, although commonly called whites, can have sulphur, yellow, red, orange or purple markings.

In the dry season their colours tend to be duller than in the wet season and some males have a tuft of hair or hair pencils to attract females. The yellows are often found near elephant dung and at certain times of the year one can witness them migrating in their thousands resembling a storm of scraps of white paper.

Blues and coppers of the *Lycaenidae* family are the largest and most complex group in Hwange and, despite their name, not all are blue and copper in colour. Many are brightly coloured, some red, others brown.

This family contains some of the smallest butterflies to be found in southern Africa and, as a result, they can be overlooked. Some have elaborate tails, an eyespot, and retractable heads which they can withdraw when resting or threatened.

The same species are also associated with ants — in a symbiotic way — ants feeding off the sweet secretion from the larvae and the larvae in turning benefiting from the ants' protection.

The last of the seven main Hwange butterfly families are *Hesperiidae* or skippers. They are robust, fast fliers, "skipping" from flower to flower which is a characteristic of the 11 species commonly found in Hwange.

Skippers are regarded as more "primitive" than other butterflies as some tend to hold their wings in a flat position rather than vertically over the back.

WHERE TO STAY

Hwange area, including Dete, Gwaai and Hwange town, has some 1,100 beds for visitors and a wide range of facilities from the more upmarket to budget accommodation, camping and caravaning.

There are several places which provide meals and beverages for visitors other than those who are staying, and petrol, ice, basic shopping, and virtually every other requirement, can be met locally. Nevertheless it is as well to be fairly self-sufficient.

In this Guide, the first comprehensive one on Hwange, we cannot list the full range of activities of each facility. Further details can be obtained by calling the number/s we have listed or checking with your travel agent.

LODGES, HOTELS AND SAFARI CAMPS

Hwange Safari Lodge
[P.B. 5792, Dete, Tel (118) 331/6, Fax (118) 337, Telex 51602 ZW]
Opened on 29 January 1972, this is Hwange's pre-eminent accommodation facility.   It is part of the extensive Zimbabwe Sun hotel, lodge and safari camp chain.   The lodge, which has 200 beds, overlooks a pumped waterhole on Hwange Estate where large herds of elephant, buffalo and many of the plains game regularly assemble.   Lions have killed within camera range. All rooms are air-conditioned with twin beds, showers, baths, toilets and telephone but, mercifully, no television. A la carte and table d'hote meals are available for guests and visitors alike, and there is a bar, swimming pool, tennis court, conference facilities and the best tourist shop in the area. There is also a same day laundry service, a fully qualified nursing sister on the staff, and baby sitters.

Baobab Hotel
[P.O. Box 120, Hwange, Tel (181) 2323, Fax (181) 3481]
Located on a hill overlooking Hwange town and the colliery, it is somewhat off the tourist beaten track, a one-hour drive from Hwange National Park. Caters mainly for visitors to the colliery.

Camp Selous
[P.O. Box 20, Gwaai, Tel (118) 2306/2101/295, Fax (118) 295]
Camp Selous, formerly known as Jabulisa, sleeps 14 people. Accommodation is in thatched twin-chalets with one double chalet/honeymoon suite. All the chalets have baths ensuite, showers and toilets. Can be accessed in a private car by turning off the Bulawayo to Victoria Falls road at Gwaai.

Chokamella Lodge
[P.O. Box 61, Dete, Tel/Fax (118) 398]
Opened in December 1992, this is one of Landela Safaris' upmarket lodges. The lodge has nine thatched bungalows and a honeymoon suite. There is mains electricity, fans in all rooms, and electric blankets for the winter months. Sleeps a maximum of 20 with peak game viewing during the dry months from May to October.

Detema Safari Lodge
[Box 69, Dete, Tel (118) 256/7, Fax (118) 269, Telex 51069]
This lodge, opened in 1993, has a 48-bed capacity in luxury tree houses and standard chalets (rondavels) under thatch. All chalets have private bath facilities with running water. Visitors may access the lodge, located on Last Hope Estate 1.5 km from Dete, by their own cars or airport pickup.

Elephant Sands Safari Lodge
[P.O. Box 52, Dete, Tel (118) 247, Fax (118) 383]
One of Hwange's newest facilities which opened in September 1995. It can be accessed by private car or transfer. Accommodation is stone and thatch with ensuite shower facilities whilst the honeymoon suite has a double bath.

Ganda Lodge
[P.O. Box 25 or 27, Dete, Tel (118) 413]
This lodge, opened in 1992, belongs to a division of the Forestry Commission. Sleeps 32 , four people in each of eight functional lodges which overlook Ganda Pan, floodlit at night, from which the lodge takes its name. The lodges are two-storey with a bath, shower and toilet downstairs. Caters for visitors as well as residents.

Gwaai River Hotel
[P.O. Box 9, Gwaai, Tel (118) 355, Fax (118) 268]
This hotel has a distinctly rustic charm. The original structure went up in the early 1940s. A decade later, over four decades ago, it was bought by Harold and Sylvia Broomberg who, now helped by various

relatives, continue to run it. The Broombergs have become an institution now catering for the grandchildren of some of their earliest visitors. Set on the bank of the Gwaai River amidst hardwood, mopane and riverine forest, the hotel can sleep 90 people in basic ensuite accommodation.

Gwaai Valley Safaris/Nyati Lodge
[P.O. Box 17, Gwaai, Tel (118) 3401, Fax (118) 268]
Specialises in photographic and touring safaris, mainly in nearby Hwange National Park and to Victoria Falls. Accommodation options range from self-catering to full board. Game drives are in open safari vehicles and transfers by mini-bus. Nearby Nyati Lodge overlooks the Shangani River valley.

Halfway House Hotel
[P.O. Box 6, Gwaai, Tel/Fax (189) 281]
Situated 220 km from Bulawayo on the Victoria Falls road this hotel can accommodate 26 people in ensuite hotel-type rooms and chalets and also provides camping facilities. It provides a 24-hour fuel service and has a kiosk, restaurant, bar and take-away.

Ivory Lodge
[P.O Box 55, Dete, Tel (118) 224, Fax (19) 65499]
This lodge, one of two (the other is Detema) in which United Touring Company (UTC) has shares, sleeps 20 in 10 raised tree-houses which have ground-level hot showers, toilets and handbasins. It is located 15 minutes from Hwange Airport and access is by private vehicle (with prior permission), or transfer. The Red Waterhole is located in front of the lodge providing spectacular close-up viewing. No children under the age of 12.

Jijima
[P.O. Box 15, Gwaai, Tel (113) 4219, Fax (113) 4349]
Built on a private estate on the eastern boundary of Hwange National Park, Jijima is a prime wildlife-viewing area away from the main tourist routes. The chalets, which sleep two people, are large and airy, being tent-under-thatch with ensuite facilities and each has a sweeping view of Jijima vlei and waterhole. The owners, Wild Horizons, are particularly noted for their birding safaris employing one of the country's foremost ornithologists, Dr Kit Hustler, as a guide.

Kalambeza Lodge
[P.O. Box 28, Gwaai, Tel (118) 2107, Fax (113) 4644]
To reach this lodge (which can be done by private car or transfer), the

visitor turns left at the 239 km peg from Bulawayo on the Victoria Falls road. Accommodation is in thatched A-frame chalets with double or twin beds ensuite. The lodge sleeps 14 visitors who should be fully self-equipped as there is no shop.

Kanondo Tree Camp
[P.Bag 6, Hillside, Bulawayo, Tel (19) 44566/7, 44569, Fax (19) 44696]
This has six tree houses constructed of wood and thatch. All have hurricane-lamp lighting with a toilet, basin and shower at ground level. Situated close to Kanondo waterhole, there is good game viewing in the area. Children under 13 years and private cars are not admitted.

Katshana Tree Lodge
[Touch the Wild, same details as Kanondo]
It is in the accommodation area where one feels the luxury of Katshana, which means "far away". The six thatch-over-teak tree lodges have African print duvets on the twin-beds, rich red-brown comfortable teak chairs and tables, and mains-lit coach lamps on the walls. The bathroom contains a full length bath, shower compartment, handbasin, toilet and alcoves for cloths.

Kumuna Lodge
[P.O. Box 19 Gwaai, Tel (118) 2308/2101 and 295, Fax (118) 295]
This family lodge sleeps 44 people in family, double and twin stone-under-thatch rondavels with ensuite showers and toilets. Access, by private car or transfer, is through Gwaai.

Main Camp
[Bookings for all National Parks facilities are done by the Central Booking Office, P.O. Box CY826, Causeway, Harare, Tel (4) 706077/8, Fax 726089, or through the Bulawayo booking agent, P.O. Box 2283, Bulawayo, Tel (19) 63646]

This is the heart of the Hwange National Park where the headquarters and main entrance is located. Lodges, cottages and chalets, sleeping between two and four people, offer a total of 118 beds. These facilities include electricity, bathrooms and toilets, bedding, towels, crockery, cutlery, cooker, fridge and other basics. There is also unlimited camping and parking for caravans with water facilities, and picnic sites. Park hours are dawn to dusk and no hitchhiking, leaving the game viewing roads, or getting out of one's vehicle is allowed in the park. ANIMALS, says the Park's instructions in bold letters, ALWAYS HAVE THE RIGHT OF WAY.

Malindi Station Lodge

[P.O. Box 72, Dete, Tel (118) 2607]
This unique and luxurious lodge, which sleeps 12 in three fully restored old railway carriages, blends a rail enthusiast's paradise with the animal kingdom. The railway carriages, a reminder of the golden age of steam, have been shunted off the tracks. But the platform columns, old fire buckets and brass lamps, appear as functional as they once were.

Miombo Safaris

[P.O. Box 90, Dete, Tel/Fax (118) 395]
Nestling in miombo woodland and sharing a common boundary with Hwange National Park, this is a small personalised bush camp run by Paul and Val de Montille. It caters for those seeking a balance between comfort, adventure and close encounters with big game.

Robins Camp

[Same details as Main Camp. Direct Tel (181) 270220]
This is the National Parks northernmost camp, located 48 km from Victoria Falls on the main Bulawayo road and 68 km from the tar down a dirt road. Robins has 22 chalets which sleep two people in each and three lodges which accommodate six people in each. Lodges have internal cooking facilities, chalets external. There is a camping and caravan site at Nantwich 11 km away. Deka exclusive camp is 25 km west of Robins. It sleeps 12, preferably family/friends in two units. Four-wheel drive is recommended.

Sable Valley Lodge

[Touch the Wild, same details as Kanondo]
Sable Valley sleeps 22 people in 11 double and twin-bed lodges. It is a small luxury lodge in a high density game area and can only be accessed by transfer. The spacious lodges are constructed of brick and thatch built under large teak trees close to a waterhole. The lodges have a shower or bath, toilet, handbasin, wall-to-wall carpeting, generator electricity and solar lighting.

Sabona Tours

[P.O. Box 73, Dete, Tel (118) 263 and 400, Fax (118) 255]
This is one of Hwange's newest operations run by Jed Moyo, an experienced professional guide who prior to opening Sabona Tours spent many years working in hotels and the parks department. Sabona (which in the Sindebele language means "hello") Tours is one of the operators helping to fill a market gap catering for the more budget-conscious end of the market.

Sikumi Tree Lodge

[Touch the Wild, same details as Kanondo]

Set at the end of the Dete vlei overlooking a waterhole notable for its prolific game viewing, this lodge is the largest of those owned by Touch the Wild and Zimbabwe Sun Hotels. There are four grades of tree lodges, double-bedded, twin-bedded, family and luxury. Situated on a private estate adjoining Hwange National Park, the tree lodges are made of thatch and wood using timber typical of the Dete area. One lodge has been specially designed to give easy access for disabled people. These tree houses have showers, toilets and basins, wall-to-wall carpeting, electric sockets (square 13 amp, 220v).

Simba Lodge

[167 Enterprise Road, Chispite, Harare, Tel/Fax (4) 495057]

Simba Lodge sleeps 12 people in twin-beds in six sandstone and thatch cottages. Access to the lodge is by air or road and the lodge can be reached in a private car as well as by transfer. It is located 222 km from Bulawayo.

Sinamatella Camp

[Details same as Main Camp]

A resident guide described Sinamatella as Hwange's best-kept secret and after visiting it there is no denying that contention. Twenty chalets, each able to sleep four, line the high bluff on either side of a restaurant appropriately called the Elephant and Dassie in acknowledgement of these two closely related but very different species. The chalets have all basic requirements like those at Main Camp to which one can drive through the park so long as you leave by 1400. The turn off for Sinamatella is just beyond Hwange town on the Bulawayo side. From the main road it is 45 km down a dirt road. An hour's drive out of Sinamatella over a somewhat rough road (four-wheel drive is recommended) is Bumbusi where there is an exclusive camp sleeping a dozen people and the Bumbusi Ruins (see precolonial history section).

Singing Bird Tours

[P.O. Box 84, Dete, Tel (118) 255, Fax (118) 383]

This new African-owned and managed company began in 1996 with the initial idea of operating a curio shop in Dete. It now provides game drives, car hire, walking safaris and budget (backpacker) accommodation. The budget accommodation is in two categories, hostels and furnished houses, both self-serviced.

The Hide

[P.O. Box GD 305, Greendale, Harare, Tel (4) 498548, 495650, Fax (4) 498265]

Very considerable care and thought has obviously gone into the construction of The Hide and its facilities. Unlike most operators it produces a field checklist of mammals, birds, common reptiles and trees. Its maximum sleeping number is 16 in luxury tents under thatch and the individual tents have ensuite showers, toilets and handbasins. Camera mounts are set into the viewing window of the carpeted ground level hide which is elephant proofed having been tested by a full grown elephant standing on top of the concrete and metal structure. The central feature is a slender two storey thatch A-frame dining room with a solid teak dining table laid with cut glass and silverware.

Umkombo Safari Lodge

[P.O. Box 10, Gwaai, Tel (118) 321, Fax (118) 268]

This lodge can accommodate up to 20 people in elevated thatched cottages which are all ensuite. The lodges are on stilts acting as an air-conditioner in the hotter months and helping the visitor to keep warm in the colder months. It is at the entrance to the Gwaai Conservancy which borders on Hwange National Park.

Caravans and Camping

There are four main caravan and camping areas in Hwange, one at the caravan park on Larami Ranch, which belongs to Mr H.G. de Vreis (P.O.Box 19, Gwaai, telephone 118-2101) and the others within the park at Main, Sinamatella and Robins camps.

FACILITIES

Walking

In wildlife areas a walker/s must be accompanied by a professional guide. Guides can be booked at National Park offices and walks, including close approaches to animals, are done by most safari camps. Always follow your guide's instructions.

Fishing

There are a number of good places in Hwange District and its environs to fish. These include rivers and dams, Mlibizi, Binga and Lake Kariba.

Golf

Some people simply cannot get away from the course and for them

Hwange Safari Lodge is a member of the Wankie Colliery course, enabling guests to play.

Doctors and hospitals
A number of places where you may stay, such as Hwange Safari Lodge and Sikumi Tree Lodge, have qualified nursing staff on the premises. Hwange Safari Lodge has a well-stocked clinic including life-support systems and oxygen. It is also a member of the Medical Air Rescue Services (MARS) scheme which means that patients in need of treatment can be airlifted out from Hwange Airport. Other cases can be referred to the modern Wankie Colliery Hospital 45 minutes away. A doctor also calls regularly at Hwange Safari Lodge.

Fuel
Petrol and diesel can be obtained at Hwange Safari Lodge, Main Camp, Halfway House, Gwaai, Dete and Hwange. Motorists are advised to keep their cars well topped up.

Ice
This can be obtained from the garage at Main Camp and also from Hwange Safari Lodge.

Hire vehicles and buses
United Touring Company/Hertz maintains a vehicle hire facility at Hwange Safari Lodge. UTC also operates a service to the airport, which it manages, and to Dete railway station. This is not a scheduled service and is based upon demand.

Shops
The Hwange Safari Lodge has a fairly well-stocked shop on the premises where the visitor can buy film, batteries, safari clothes, souvenirs, books and postcards. Main Camp also has a curio shop as well as a shop selling most basics.

Camera equipment and binoculars
Hwange Safari Lodge rents binoculars but supply is limited. There is nowhere to rent camera equipment. Film and batteries are available in adequate quantities at Hwange Safari Lodge and Main Camp but visitors are advised to carry supplies, particularly for video equipment.

Restaurants
Hwange Safari Lodge caters for visitors, and more downmarket is the restaurant at Main Camp and the Elephant and Dassie at Sinamatella where squirrels may share your food.

CHECKLIST OF THE MAIN MAMMALS OF HWANGE

* Denotes possibility of being seen at certain times of the year

Pangolin
Vervet Monkey
Spotted Hyena
Bateared Fox
Blackbacked Jackal
Slender Mongoose
Dwarf Mongoose
Leopard
Caracal*
Serval*
Elephant
White Rhinoceros*
Warthog
Giraffe
Steenbok
Klipspringer*
Waterbuck
Gemsbok*
Sable
Cape Hartebeest*
Kudu
Eland

Baboon
Brown Hyena
Painted Hunting Dog
Sidestriped Jackal
Honey Badger
Banded Mongoose
Cheetah
Lion
Wild Cat*
Yellowspotted Dassie
Black Rhinoceros*
Zebra
Hippopotamus
Common Duiker
Sharpe's Grysbok*
Reedbuck*
Impala
Roan*
Tsessebe*
Blue Wildebeest
Bushbuck
Buffalo

CHECKLIST OF BIRDS OF HWANGE

All numbers used are taken from Roberts' *Guide to Birds of Southern Africa.* This list was compiled by Dr Kit Hustler of Wild Horizons, PO Box 159, Victoria Falls, Zimbabwe (Tel: 263 (13) 4219) and Mr Peter Ginn of Peter Ginn Birding Safaris, PO Box 44, Marondera, Zimbabwe (Tel/Fax: 263 (79) 23411). This is not a definitive list of birds found in the Hwange area but a general guide to what can be seen.

No.	Bird Name	No.	Bird Name
001	Ostrich	084	Black Stork
008	Dabchick	085	Abdim's Stork
058	Reed Cormorant	086	Woollynecked Stork
060	Darter	087	African Openbill
062	Grey Heron	088	Saddlebilled Stork
064	Goliath Heron	089	Marabou Stork
065	Purple Heron	095	African Spoonbill
066	Great White Egret	099	Whitefaced Duck
067	Little Egret	102	Egyptian Goose
071	Cattle Egret	115	Knobbilled Duck
081	Hamerkop	116	Spurwinged Goose
083	White Stork	118	Secretary Bird

No.	Bird Name	No.	Bird Name
121	Hooded Vulture	297	Spotted Dikkop
123	Whitebacked Vulture	298	Water Dikkop
124	Lappetfaced Vulture	300	Temminck's Courser
125	Whiteheaded Vulture	302	Threebanded Courser
126a	Black Kite	338	Whiskered Tern
126b	Yellowbilled Kite	339	Whitewinged Tern
127	Blackshouldered Kite	347	Doublebanded Sandgrouse
131	Black Eagle	352	Redeyed Dove
132	Tawny Eagle	354	Cape Turtle Dove
135	Wahlberg's Eagle	355	Laughing Dove
137	African Hawk Eagle	356	Namaqua Dove
140	Martial Eagle	358	Greenspotted Dove
142	Brown Snake Eagle	361	Green Pigeon
143	Blackbreasted Snake Eagle	364	Meyer's Parrot
146	Bateleur	373	Grey Lourie
148	African Fish Eagle	375	African Cuckoo
149	Steppe Buzzard	377	Redchested Cuckoo
154	Lizard Buzzard	381	Striped Cuckoo
157	Little Sparrowhawk	382	Jacobin Cuckoo
159	Little Banded Goshawk	385	Klaas's Cuckoo
161	Gabar Goshawk	388	Black Coucal
163	Dark Chanting Goshawk	392	Barn Owl
169	Gymnogene	396	Scops Owl
173	Hobby Falcon	397	Whitefaced Owl
180	Eastern Redfooted Kestrel	398	Pearlspotted Owl
183	Lesser Kestrel	399	Barred Owl
185	Dickinson's Kestrel	401	Spotted Eagle Owl
188	Coqui Francolin	402	Giant Eagle Owl
189	Crested Francolin	405	Fierynecked Nightjar
194	Redbilled Francolin	421	Palm Swift
199	Swainson's Francolin	426	Redfaced Mousebird
201	Harlequin Quail	428	Pied Kingfisher
203	Helmeted Guineafowl	429	Giant Kingfisher
205	Kurrichane Buttonquail	431	Malachite Kingfisher
209	Crowned Crane	432	Pygmy Kingfisher
213	Blake Crake	433	Woodland Kingfisher
226	Moorhen	435	Brownhooded Kingfisher
230	Kori Bustard	436	Greyhooded Kingfisher
237	Redcrested Korhaan	437	Striped Kingfisher
240	African Jacana	438	European Bee-eater
249	Threebanded Plover	441	Carmine Bee-eater
255	Crowned Plover	444	Little Bee-eater
258	Blacksmith Plover	445	Swallowtailed Bee-eater
260	Wattled Plover	446	European Roller
264	Common Sandpiper	447	Lilacbreasted Roller
266	Wood Sandpiper	449	Purple Roller
270	Greenshank	450	Broadbilled Roller
295	Blackwinged Stilt	451	Hoopoe

No.	Bird Name	No.	Bird Name
452	Redbilled Hoopoe	621	Titbabbler
454	Greater Scimitarbill	643	Willow Warbler
457	Grey Hornbill	651	Longbilled Crombec
458	Redbilled Hornbill	653	Yellowbellied Eremomela
459	Sthn Yellowbilled Hornbill	656	Burntnecked Eremomela
460	Crowned Hornbill	657a	Greybacked Bleating Warbler
461	Bradfield's Hornbill	659	Stierling's Barred Warbler
463	Ground Hornbill	672	Rattling Cisticola
464	Blackcollared Barbet	681	Neddicky
465	Acacia Pied Barbet	683	Tawnyflanked Prinia
470	Yellowfronted Tinker Barbet	685	Blackchested Prinia
473	Crested Barbet	689	Spotted Flycatcher
474	Greater Honeyguide	694	Black Flycatcher
476	Lesser Honeyguide	695	Marico Flycatcher
481	Bennett's Woodpecker	701	Chinspot Batis
483	Goldentailed Woodpecker	710	Paradise Flycatcher
486	Cardinal Woodpecker	711	African Pied Wagtail
487	Bearded Woodpecker	731	Lesser Grey Shrike
494	Rufousnaped Lark	733	Redbacked Shrike
496	Flappet Lark	735	Longtailed Shrike
507	Redcapped Lark	737	Tropical Boubou Shrike
515	Chestnutbacked Finchlark	739	Crimsonbreasted Shrike
518	European Swallow	740	Puffback Shrike
524	Redbreasted Swallow	743	Threestreaked Tchagra
527	Lesser Striped Swallow	744	Blackcrowned Tachgra
531	Greyrumped Swallow	748	Orangebreasted Bush Shrike
538	Black Cuckooshrike	751	Greyheaded Bush Shrike
539	Whitebreasted Cuckooshrike	753	White Helmetshrike
541	Forktailed Drongo	754	Redbilled Helmetshrike
543	European Golden Oriole	756	Whitecrowned Shrike
544	African Golden Oriole	760	Wattled Starling
545	Blackheaded Oriole	761	Plumcoloured Starling
548	Pied Crow	763	Longtailed Starling
554	Southern Black Tit	764	Glossy Starling
558	Grey Penduline Tit	769	Redwinged Starling
560	Arrowmarked Babbler	771	Yellowbilled Oxpecker
563	Pied Babbler	772	Redbilled Oxpecker
567	Redeyed Bulbul	779	Marico Sunbird
568	Blackeyed Bulbul	787	Whitebellied Sunbird
569	Terrestrial Bulbul	791	Scarletchested Sunbird
574	Yellowbellied Bulbul	792	Black Sunbird
576	Kurrichane Thrush	797	Yellow White-eye
580	Groundscraper Thrush	798	Redbilled Buffalo Weaver
587	Capped Wheatear	801	House Sparrow
593	Arnot's Chat	804	Greyheaded Sparrow
599	Heuglin's Robin	805	Yellowthroated Sparrow
613	Whitebrowed Robin	806	Scalyfeathered Finch
615	Kalahari Robin	811	Spottedbacked Weaver

No.	Bird Name	No.	Bird Name
814	Masked Weaver	847	Blackcheeked Waxbill
816	Golden Weaver	855	Cutthroat Finch
819	Redheaded Weaver	861	Shafttailed Whydah
821	Redbilled Quelea	862	Paradise Whydah
824	Red Bishop	865	Purple Widowfinch
829	Whitewinged Widow	867	Steelblue Widowfinch
834	Melba Finch	869	Yelloweyed Canary
841	Jameson's Firefinch	870	Blackthroated Canary
842	Redbilled Firefinch	881	Streakyheaded Canary
844	Blue Waxbill	884	Goldenbreasted Bunting
845	Violeteared Waxbill	886	Rock Bunting

CHECKLIST OF TREES AND SHRUBS OF HWANGE

This list was taken from the "Victoria Falls and Hwange" section of *Keys to the Trees of Zimbabwe* by Meg Coates Palgrave, PO Box 4643, Harare, Zimbabwe (Tel: 263 (4) 742 765 Fax: 263 (4) 742 800)

TREE/SHRUB NAME	BOTANICAL NAME
African Wattle	Peltophorum africanum
Albida	Faidherbia albida
Azanza	Azanza garckeana
Blade Thorn	Acacia fleckii
Buffalo-thorn	Ziziphus mucronata
Burkea	Burkea africana
Camel Thorn	Acacia erioloba
Crocodile-bark	Diospyros quiloensis
Diamond-leaved Euclea	Euclea divinorum
Donkeyberry	Grewia flavescens
Duikerberry	Pseudolachnostylis maprouneifolia
Ebony Dalbergia	Dalbergia melanoxylon
Ebony Diospyros	Diospyros mespiliformis
Flame Thorn	Acacia ataxacantha
Glossy Combretum	Combretum apiculatum
Golden Bean Tree	Markhamia obtusifolia
Gummy Gardenia	Gardenia resiniflua
Jasmine Pea	Baphia massaiensis
Jesse-Bush Combretum	Combretum celastroides
Kalahari Sand Terminalia	Terminalia brachystemma
Kirkia	Kirkia acuminata
Knobby Bridelia	Bridelia cathartica
Large-fruited Combretum	Combretum zeyheri
Large Jesse-Bush	Combretum elaeagnoides
Large Sourplum	Ximenia caffra
Leadwood	Combretum imberbe
Manketti Nut	Schinziophyton rautanenii
Mopane	Colophospermum mopane
Mouse-eared Combretum	Combretum hereroense
Mukwa	Pterocarpus angolensis